DATE			

UNDERSTANDING
REYNOLDS PRICE

Understanding Contemporary American Literature
Matthew J. Bruccoli, General Editor

Volumes on

Edward Albee • John Barth • Donald Barthelme • The Beats
The Black Mountain Poets • Robert Bly • Raymond Carver
Chicano Literature • Contemporary American Drama
Contemporary American Horror Fiction
Contemporary American Science Fiction • James Dickey
E. L. Doctorow • John Gardner • George Garrett • John Hawkes
Joseph Heller • John Irving • Randall Jarrell • William Kennedy
Ursula K. Le Guin • Denise Levertov • Bernard Malamud
Carson McCullers • Arthur Miller • Toni Morrison's Fiction
Vladimir Nabokov • Joyce Carol Oates • Tim O'Brien
Flannery O'Connor • Cynthia Ozick • Walker Percy
Katherine Anne Porter • Reynolds Price • Thomas Pynchon
Theodore Roethke • Philip Roth • Mary Lee Settle
Isaac Bashevis Singer • Gary Snyder • William Stafford
Anne Tyler • Kurt Vonnegut • Tennessee Williams

UNDERSTANDING
Reynolds
PRICE

JAMES A. SCHIFF

UNIVERSITY OF SOUTH CAROLINA PRESS

Published in Columbia, South Carolina, by the
University of South Carolina Press

Manufactured in the United States of America

00 99 98 97 96   5 4 3 2 1

Some of the material used in this book originally appeared in my essay
"Fathers and Sons in the Fiction of Reynolds Price: A Sense of Crucial
Ambiguity," *Southern Review* 29.1 (Winter 1993): 16–29. I am indebted
to the Harriet Wasserman Literary Agency, Inc., and to Scribner, an
imprint of Simon & Schuster, Inc., for their permission to quote from the
following works by Reynolds Price:
The Surface of Earth. © 1975 by Reynolds Price. Reprinted with
permission of Scribner, an imprint of Simon & Schuster, Inc.
The Source of Light. © 1981 by Reynolds Price. Reprinted with permission of Scribner, an imprint of Simon & Schuster, Inc.
Clear Pictures. © 1988, 1989 by Reynolds Price. Reprinted with
permission of Scribner, an imprint of Simon & Schuster, Inc.
A Whole New Life. © 1982, 1986, 1990, 1994 by Reynolds Price. Reprinted
with permission of Scribner, an imprint of Simon & Schuster, Inc.

Library of Congress Cataloging-in-Publication Data will be found at
the end of this book.

For Walker and Beth

CONTENTS

EDITOR'S PREFACE

The volumes of *Understanding Contemporary American Literature* have been planned as guides or companions for students as well as good nonacademic readers. The editor and publisher perceive a need for these volumes because much of the influential contemporary literature makes special demands. Uninitiated readers encounter difficulty in approaching works that depart from the traditional forms and techniques of prose and poetry. Literature relies on conventions, but the conventions keep evolving; new writers form their own conventions—which in time may become familiar. Put simply, *UCAL* provides instruction in how to read certain contemporary writers—identifying and explicating their material, themes, use of language, point of view, structures, symbolism, and responses to experience.

The word *understanding* in the titles was deliberately chosen. Many willing readers lack an adequate understanding of how contemporary literature works; that is, what the author is attempting to express and the means by which it is conveyed. Although the criticism and analysis in the series have been aimed at a level of general accessibility, these introductory volumes are meant to be applied in conjunction with the works they cover. They do not provide a substitute for the works and authors they introduce, but rather prepare the reader for more profitable literary experiences.

M. J. B.

ACKNOWLEDGMENTS

I wish to thank Sallie and Raymond Harris, Jr., of Macon, North Carolina, for the wonderful hospitality and kindness, not to mention the grand tour. For their assistance with my research, thanks go to Melissa Delbridge and the Special Collections Library at Duke University; the interlibrary loan people at Langsam Library at the University of Cincinnati; Connie Cussen and Wayne Godwin at Channel 48, WCET-TV in Cincinnati; and Daniel L. Daily, William King, and the Duke University Archives. I also wish to thank David Hicks for his many helpful suggestions.

On the homefront, Bruni Robles, whose energy and curiosity are contagious, made it possible for me to work at home, and I am grateful. Many thanks also go to Robert and Adele Schiff, who have continuously provided support and love. The greatest and deepest thanks, however, are to Beth and Walker, who continue to endure my many hours behind books and computer screens, seldom questioning or complaining—the patience and love of saints.

Finally, I wish to thank to Reynolds Price, who generously provided books, answered more questions than any human being should tolerate, and was always helpful and encouraging.

UNDERSTANDING
REYNOLDS PRICE

CHAPTER ONE

Understanding Reynolds Price

Career

In the life of Reynolds Price, as in his work, events have a way of swelling with mystery and significance to almost biblical proportions. Consider Price's birth in the small rural town of Macon, North Carolina, on 1 February 1933. The delivery of Elizabeth Price's first child had become so difficult—the child "was breeched" in the womb—that the family physician reported to Elizabeth's husband, "I'm losing them both."[1] The husband, Will Price, a salesman, then fled the house, went to the woodshed, and there, according to family legend (and in the words of Price the novelist), "sealed a bargain with God, as stark and unbreakable as any blood pact in Genesis—if Elizabeth lived, and the child, he'd never drink again."[2] Elizabeth and the child, Edward Reynolds Price, survived, and though the "family myth" credits Will with giving up alcohol, Price himself emends the story by saying of his father, "the fact is, in time he did but not at once."[3]

Whether or not this account of Price's birth is fully accurate, it provides an appropriate beginning for a writer whose life and work have been viewed as bold, singular, and mysterious. The story also helps to explain Price's bond with his father and his more general fascination with relationships between fathers and sons—particularly with the story of Abraham and Isaac, in which Price, like Isaac, is gift and hostage in a divine pact. Ultimately, the story demonstrates, at least in part, why virtually no action is inconsequential or without ramifications in the life and work of

Reynolds Price. Through an intense watchfulness, a grand manner of telling, and belief in a larger sense of design, Price bestows meaning. A husband's vow to change his ways during his wife's dangerous childbirth is hardly unheard of, yet Price's birth story becomes compelling because the author himself boldly raises it to the level of myth, alluding to Genesis and utilizing such language as "blood pact" and "sealed a bargain with God."

Perhaps the most useful and dominant fact of Price's childhood is his bond with his parents, of whom he speaks with unusual admiration and affection: "They were almost too lovable. . . . my brother and I . . . have all our lives been handicapped by the fact that we seldom meet human beings as loyal, affectionate or continuously amusing as our parents were."[4] Certainly this early bond with his parents—what Price has written of as a "triad," or three-way marriage (Price was an only child until he was eight)—has been one of the most significant relationships in his life and has played a central role in his writing. The novelist Anne Tyler, an early student of Price's at Duke University, remarks how she realized from Price's "naturally happy" state and his "serene and gravely trusting" face that "*he must have been a very much loved child.*"[5] In addition to his parents and later a younger brother, Price was fortunate to live in the midst of an extended family of cousins, aunts, and uncles who were not only supportive but were also wonderful talkers and storytellers.

Yet his childhood and early adolescence, spent in small North Carolina towns (Macon, Henderson, Warrenton, Roxboro, Asheboro), were not without problems. His early years were marred by illness (allergic rashes, frightening seizures); his family moved an average of once a year until he entered high school; family finances in these Depression years were always tight (at one point the family had to give up their home because Will could not come up with a fifty-dollar payment); and there were continual fears, on Price's part, that his father would return to drinking and that Price would wind up an orphan.

In addition, Price's atypical early interests and artistic nature led to occasional isolation and torment from his peers. Whereas other children played baseball, Price painted, listened to opera, collected books, and according to his brother, "conceived grand designs such as filming a version of 'The Song of Bernadette' with a cast drawn from our neighborhood."[6] Price was hardly the typical child, and during his early adolescent years in Warrenton, a time which was mostly miserable, he experienced rejection, betrayal, and even physical beatings from his peers. Though a traumatic adolescence is not so unusual, what is interesting in Price's case is how his rejection by the town children of Warrenton "forced [him] to seek friendship among the bussed-in farm children."[7] These rural children who accepted him would later become the models for the central characters in much of his early fiction (*A Long and Happy Life, A Generous Man*); as Price explains, "the openfaced kindness they showed me . . . and the facts they taught me about a life lived close to the ground in merciless weather—it all poured deep into my storage cellars and slept for years."[8]

A precocious adolescent with unusual interests, Price found a niche for himself in the classroom, where he was inspired by a string of good teachers to continue developing his abilities in the arts. Though music and art were strong early passions, Price realized by the time he was at Broughton High School in Raleigh that as a visual artist he would never be more than a "copyist," and so he turned to writing, primarily poetry.

From Broughton, Price went on to nearby Duke University, where he won a full scholarship and thrived. Says Price, "I loved being in college. It was the first time in my life when the things I was good at were prized by the place I was in."[9] At Duke, Price became editor of the literary magazine, wrote his first real story ("Michael Egerton"), and met and had his work evaluated by visiting writers Elizabeth Bowen and Eudora Welty. Welty, in fact, called Price's first story "professional" and asked if she could send it to her agent.

Graduating Phi Beta Kappa and summa cum laude from Duke, Price won a Rhodes scholarship and entered Merton College, Oxford University, where he studied seventeenth-century English literature, concentrating upon Milton. In his three years at Oxford he produced a thesis on Milton's *Samson Agonistes,* several short stories which would later appear in *The Names and Faces of Heroes* (1963), and the plan for a first novel, *A Long and Happy Life* (1962). In regard to his early fiction, Price found English magazines more receptive than American, and in effect his career was launched overseas. In 1958 Price realized his first major publication when Stephen Spender's *Encounter* accepted his short story "A Chain of Love."

In that same year Price returned to Duke to teach in the English department and has remained there ever since. Typically he teaches one semester a year—a course in writing and one in Milton, although recently he has taught the Gospels as literature. Stories of his teaching are legendary, and he has affected and influenced many younger writers: Anne Tyler, Josephine

UNDERSTANDING REYNOLDS PRICE

Humphreys, Wallace Kaufman, David Guy, Fred Chappell, James Applewhite, Charlie Smith. Novelist Humphreys, who studied with Price in the mid-1960s, describes him as "as darkly handsome as Elvis Presley" and writes: "I loved him, and so I learned from him; I believe that's how most true learning occurs. When I left Duke, I felt it a great loss that I would not hear him again."[10]

As for why he returned to and has remained in North Carolina after his years in England, Price explains: "This part of North Carolina is where 95 percent of my emotional intensity has been grounded. My early childhood familial experiences, and all my later intense emotional experiences have occurred here. . . . Also, from my point of view, I'm the world's authority on this place. It's the place about which I have perfect pitch."[11] For a child who moved so often, home becomes a significant place, and since 1958 Price has lived in the same rolling, wooded countryside of Orange County, between Durham and Chapel Hill.

Price's arrival as an important young writer came in 1962 with the publication of his first novel, *A Long and Happy Life,* which appeared simultaneously as a volume from Atheneum and as a work in its entirety in *Harper's.* The novel, which traces the troubled love of Rosacoke Mustian and Wesley Beavers, won the William Faulkner Foundation Award for a notable first novel, received extraordinary critical praise, and has gone on to sell more than a million copies and to be translated into fourteen languages.

Price followed this initial success with two volumes that likewise received much critical praise: a short story collection, *The Names and Faces of Heroes* (1963), and a novel, *A Generous*

Man (1966). Together with *A Long and Happy Life,* these three volumes account for what some have called Price's "Mustian Period"—Mustian being the rural North Carolina family which dominated Price's fiction for approximately eleven years (1955–1966).

The publication of Price's next two books, *Love and Work* (1968) and *Permanent Errors* (1970), marks a new phase in his work and reveals a departure in character, tone, and style. Price's characters are no longer the rural farm children he encountered in his youth; rather, his protagonist in these works is most often a well-educated and highly self-conscious writer. Unlike the earlier works, these two volumes give the impression of being more closely autobiographical. In addition they are darker and graver than the earlier novels, though this earlier work is hardly the comic romp that many reviewers described. Finally, Price's style, particularly as he turns toward reading and translating biblical narrative during this period, becomes spare, dense, and severe. As Michael Kreyling explains, "The style of the prose becomes almost hieroglyphic; image, symbol, scene, dialogue, are set flush against each other with a minimum of prosaic mortar and ornament."[12] Though these two more demanding volumes met with little of the popular success attained by Price's earlier writings, they are certainly more peculiar and disturbing works.

The culmination of Price's second phase of writing, from 1966 to 1984, is the publication of the first two volumes of his most significant achievement to date, the Mayfield trilogy, collectively titled *A Great Circle* and individually *The Surface of Earth* (1975), *The Source of Light* (1981), and *The Promise of Rest* (1995). Price had begun work on *The Surface of Earth* as

UNDERSTANDING REYNOLDS PRICE

early as 1961 but was "balked" in his attempt for more than a decade. His translation of biblical stories, begun during the late 1960s and early 1970s (a collection of these translations, entitled *A Palpable God,* was published in 1978), played some role in Price's finally being able to write his most ambitious novel, *The Surface of Earth.* In this novel one can see not only the influence of biblical themes, characters, and style, but also a synthesis of characteristics from earlier work: the fixed sense of place and the focus on family relationships from his Mustian novels integrate with more recent innovations in style (greater compression and introspection) and theme (an almost biblical interest in a family's development over generations).

One critic has called this second phase of Price's career his "stoic" period,[13] though the term *self-reflective* may more accurately define these years. The central character in Price's major works of fiction during this period—Thomas Eborn, Charles Tamplin, Hutch Mayfield—is a rather introspective writer who, while not Price himself, bears a certain resemblance to the author. In addition to the works of fiction and translation he produced during these years, Price fully established himself as a "man of letters" by publishing a volume of essays, *Things Themselves* (1972); a play, *Early Dark* (1977); a volume of poetry, *Vital Provisions* (1982); and a commissioned television play, *Private Contentment* (1984).

The next phase of Price's writing is signaled by the most dramatic change in his life. In the late spring of 1984, when he was approximately one-third finished with the manuscript of *Kate Vaiden,* Price began experiencing problems walking. After entering Duke Hospital for tests, he soon learned of a "pencil-thick and gray-colored" tumor, ten inches long and cancerous, which was "intricately braided in the core of [his] spinal cord."[14] Immediate surgery was called for, and though his spinal cord survived the daylong ordeal intact, the surgery failed to remove more than ten percent of the growth. Price's prognosis was bleak, with paralysis and death appearing imminent.

The next step was heavy doses of radiation over a five-week period. During this time Price's legs continued to deteriorate, and soon after, he became a paraplegic. In 1985 he entered a rehabilitation program where he learned to navigate and survive in a wheelchair; however, in the ensuing months, his pain increased steadily while doctors prescribed more and more drugs. Eventually it took two further radical surgeries in 1986, along with help from biofeedback and hypnosis to relieve the intense pain, before Price was able to return to a productive and "relatively" normal life of writing, teaching, and travel. Yet it was hardly his old life. Confined to a wheelchair and dependent upon an assistant to help with the chores of life, Price, who had always lived alone by choice, was now leading a vastly different existence. As far as he was concerned, the old Reynolds Price was dead, as "dead as any teen-aged Marine drilled through the forehead in an Asian jungle."[15] However, once he had weathered what he calls the "eye of the storm," the time between the spring of 1984 and the fall of 1988, Price writes, surprisingly, his life actually became "better." Though he admits that the word *better* perhaps carries "the stench of sentimentality, narcissism, blind optimism or lunacy," he explains that his new life is better in "two measurable ways": paraplegia has made him a more patient and watchful person and a dramatically more prolific writer.[16] In addition, his annual MRI scans continue to show his spine clear of cancer.

UNDERSTANDING REYNOLDS PRICE

Initially the illness prevented Price from writing, but after receiving a commission in the fall of 1984 from Hendrix College in Arkansas to compose a play, he began a prolific burst which has yet to cease and which he attributes to three causes: released time from life's chores, now that he has employed an assistant; sublimation of sexual energy into his work (a lifelong bachelor, Price writes of eroticism's playing a large and intense role in his life); and acquisition of a word processor. In nine years (1986–1995), Price published fourteen books—five novels, two volumes of memoirs, two volumes of poetry, two collections of plays, two collections of stories, and a collection of essays. By comparison the "old Price," though never a slow worker, took twenty-two years (1962–1984) to publish his first twelve volumes.

In addition to writing faster, Price, in the eyes of many, was also writing better. *Kate Vaiden* (1986) won the National Book Critics Circle Award and became Price's most commercially and critically successful novel since *A Long and Happy Life. Clear Pictures* (1989), a memoir, inspired four-time Oscar-winning filmmaker Charles Guggenheim to direct a documentary about Price's life. *New Music* (1990), a trilogy of full-length plays, won an enormous grant and was produced in its entirety by the Cleveland Play House. A second memoir, *A Whole New Life* (1994), depicting Price's battle with and recovery from cancer, led to invitations from America's major news and talk shows and generated more reader mail than Price has ever received. Finally during this period, Price emerged as perhaps the first significant American novelist to compose a successful Top 40 popular song; with his friend, singer/songwriter James Taylor, Price collaborated on the 1991 hit popular song "Copperline," as well as on another song, entitled "New Hymn."[17]

In this third phase of Price's career—his "New Life," so to speak—one sees, in addition to the prolificacy, changes in the writing itself. Price has turned toward more personal composition in this period: he has published two volumes of memoirs, a poetry journal (included in two successive volumes of poems), and personal essays dealing with religious belief, childhood, and college. In keeping, perhaps, with this more personal approach, Price, for the first time in his career, has composed novels in the first-person point of view: *Kate Vaiden, The Tongues of Angels,* and *Blue Calhoun.* The Price of recent years—as seen in his novels, short stories, memoirs, essays, poetry, even drama—is drawn to a more personal voice, a storytelling "I," who is most often a late-middle-aged southerner with a strong need to reflect upon events of the distant past. This "I" of Price's more recent work has also plunged more openly into those questions concerning religion, sexuality, gender, and race which have long been so crucial to the author.

Related to this shift toward first-person narration, one finds a change in Price's language and voice; he has become more colloquial and accessible. Since Kate Vaiden and Blue Calhoun must be convincing as human voices, Price has had to resist writing in the literarily astringent and rhetorically demanding style which characterizes such earlier works as *Love and Work* and *The Surface of Earth.* Though Price's themes and obsessions have not changed dramatically in recent years, his voice has become more personal and inviting, a fact which has led to his increased popular acceptance.

Critical Overview

Since the 1962 publication of his award-winning first novel, *A Long and Happy Life,* Reynolds Price has been a visible presence in contemporary American letters. He has gone on to publish twenty-five more books, ten of them novels, and the majority have received high praise. Stephen Spender has compared Price to Hemingway and Joyce and states that "He ranks very high, with Eudora Welty and, I suppose, Faulkner." Jefferson Humphries has written, "I don't know of any writer who has more important things to say, more really indispensable comfort and advice to offer." Lloyd Shaw and others have referred to Price as America's "best living Southern fiction writer,"[18] and authors and critics such as Anthony Burgess, Frank Kermode, Allan Gurganus, Guy Davenport, Joyce Carol Oates, Toni Morrison, and Michael Kreyling have praised his work. In addition Price has been inducted into the American Academy of Arts and Letters and, as mentioned above, been the subject of a major documentary film.

To argue then that Price has been neglected appears ludicrous, yet consider his status within the world of academic literary criticism, a world in which professors write articles and books that help to shape canons. Despite the praise from reviewers, Price has not received a great deal of scholarly attention—certainly less than other members of his literary generation, such as John Updike, Philip Roth, Thomas Pynchon, Joyce Carol Oates, Toni Morrison, John Barth, Sylvia Plath, Susan Sontag, Don DeLillo, and Cynthia Ozick (writers all born between 1928 and 1938).

UNDERSTANDING REYNOLDS PRICE

When the work of one writer receives less attention than that devoted to his peers, there is often valid reason—the writer is simply not as good. Though some may argue this is the case with Price, the lack of critical attention would appear to have more to do with cultural matters and literary fashion. As Michael Kreyling points out, "Two planetary influences shaped Southern writing in the latter days of the Southern Renascence, the late 1950s and early 1960s. . . . How does this novel match Faulkner? How does this theme advance or baffle the cause of social justice for the Negro in the South?"[19] Since the publication of his first novel, and particularly since John Wain's 1966 review of *A Generous Man,* Price has been unable, at least until recent years, to escape the first question. In his review Wain referred to Price as "a writer of obvious gifts, powers and ambitions" but added, "it is not too late to remind him that Faulkner's books have already been written."[20] Fifteen years later, in 1981, Benjamin DeMott continued this familiar line of criticism in a review of *The Source of Light* entitled "A Minor Faulkner": "The overall impression left is that of a fictional world rendered indistinct by the spreading shade of the great Faulkner tree."[21] One has only to scan the miles of interviews which Price has endured to see how often "the Faulkner question" arises.

To a large extent, one could argue that because of Faulkner male southern writers of the mid to late twentieth century, such as Price, have been subjected to a linkage and comparison that is in many cases not only mistaken but also belittling. Though contemporary American writers of the Midwest, West, and Northeast have their own literary ghosts, none is as big and as recent as Faulkner, and writers from these other regions are seldom lumped together and designated by their region in the way southern writers are.[22] Without careful scrutiny of his work, critics have placed Price under the enormous shadow of the great Mississippian simply because both are southerners. Geographically, Price's home and the area he writes about are closer to New York City than to Oxford, Mississippi, yet from the perspective of a northeastern literary establishment, North Carolina and Mississippi are joined, just as Colombia and Peru are joined and then called "Latin America." The point is not to denounce the literary establishment but rather to suggest that hasty decisions and generalizations are sometimes made about writers whose geographical status is unfamiliar. Though it is impossible for a southern writer to be unaware of Faulkner, careful examination of Price's work will reveal that the Bible, Milton, Tolstoy, and Welty—not Faulkner—are the more significant influences.

Kreyling's second inescapable question for a southern writer of Price's generation also helps to explain Price's critical reception: how does this writer's work stand in regard to its advancing "the cause of social justice for the Negro in the South"? Price's status as a southern white male during the civil rights movement did little to help his cause with literary critics across the country. In addition, Price's work, which has sometimes been labeled "old- fashioned" or "traditional," mostly ignores the pressing issues of racial hostility and equality, concerning itself instead with an earlier world in which mostly kind-hearted, nonviolent blacks serve the needs of white families.

Perhaps the main reason, though, for the lack of critical attention directed toward Price's work has to do with literary fashion. Price's career has spanned an era in American literature in which academia has been generally more receptive to writing which is clever, playful, bleak, and postmodern—the antithesis of Price's work. Throughout much of Price's early and middle career in the 1960s and 1970s, the rage was for more experimental fiction—Pynchon, Barthelme, and Barth. A writer whose influences are mostly classical, Price has never been interested in experimentalism, what he refers to as "the fiction of game and puzzle."[23] Though his work is often bold and original, Price is a traditionalist in regard to narrative technique, theme, and subject matter.

In addition, Price's prose style for much of his career, particularly during the late 1960s and 1970s, has been, in the words of Constance Rooke, "highly pronounced, unusual, and quite often difficult."[24] In an age favoring a more idiomatic, casual, and realistic prose, Price strives for an impressive sound which sometimes reminds one, more than any other example from contemporary American literature does, of the Bible or even *Paradise Lost.* Related to this is the fact that one does not find a detailed sense of the *contemporary* world in Price's writing, as one does in, say, Updike's Rabbit novels or DeLillo's *White Noise.* Those writers are expert at incorporating sociology into their narratives, utilizing, often in a metaphorical sense, a wealth of information from newspaper headlines, television programs, and social trends. Relatively speaking, Price's fiction relies little upon sociological details; there is a chiseled bareness to his vision, and his characters are depicted at the emotional core, with little regard for the trappings of contemporary life. Thus for readers eager to find detailed sociology in fiction, Price may be something of a disappointment.

UNDERSTANDING REYNOLDS PRICE

To move beyond the cultural circumstances adversely affecting Price's stature within critical circles, how does one describe his writing? To begin, *deeply rooted in time and place.* Though Price is more interested in character than setting, there is nevertheless a rich, and fixed, sense of time and place in his work. At least ninety percent of his writing is set in the small towns and rural landscapes of central/eastern North Carolina and southern Virginia. As one critic puts it, and a slight alteration has been made to account for more recent work, "the surface of Price's earth is bounded on the south by Raleigh . . . ; on the north by Richmond and Washington; on the west by [Nashville]; and on the east by the Atlantic Ocean at Virginia Beach."[25] In regard to time, Price's fiction is primarily set in the 1940s and 1950s, the period of his own adolescence and early adulthood, though occasionally he will return to the early years of the century or set an entire novel in the 1990s.

Perhaps what allows Price to concentrate so intensely on his characters and their emotional identities is that his locale is a constant—an absolutely familiar place, largely untouched by outside influence. Price creates an insular world unaffected by television or the trends and fashion of New York or Los Angeles. Though World War II hovers in the background in much of Price's fiction, his work relies little upon historical affairs or sociological details. By resisting the influence of sociology, Price offers a picture of rural familiarity which stands in direct contrast to the urban disorientation and dislocation prevalent in so many mid- to late-twentieth-century American writers, such as Barthelme and Pynchon. Though Price's characters are often in turmoil, confusion, and pain, it is not because they are out of sorts with or disoriented by a fragmented and changing environment; rather it is due to problems within themselves, primarily their inability to satisfy their inner desires and needs. As both Rooke and Jefferson Humphries have pointed out, the turmoil for Price's characters comes largely from within; they are "haunted by a double bind: the impossibility of living alone without desiring others, and the impossibility of being with others without sacrificing a large part of the self's autonomy, without mourning a (perhaps illusory) freedom."[26]

As for his characters, Price spends less time than many of his contemporaries do writing about individuals who culturally and intellectually resemble the author himself. For all of his interest in what Fred Chappell calls "high culture" (painting, opera, classical music), and despite his status as a Rhodes scholar, Price creates few characters who attend graduate school, frequent museums, or listen to opera.[27] For the most part Price's characters, with their memorable names—Rosacoke Mustian, Wesley Beavers, Blue Calhoun—are relatively unambitious small-town and rural commoners: salesmen, small-time farmers, mechanics, and secretaries. Though some critics have lamented his choice of characters, Price counters by pointing to ignorance and geographical stereotyping on their part: "My own two earliest novels got a fair amount of hillbillying when in fact they dealt with characters who live two hundred miles east of the nearest hill and are as distinct from hillfolk as from Brooklyn cabbies."[28]

Though the forces which have led Price to create such characters no doubt have more to do with unconscious need than willed choice, the characters themselves serve to dispel the stereotypical notion that rural southerners must be either ignorant provincials or sensationalized grotesques. Price never condescends to or distorts his characters but rather endows them with dignity, humor, wit, and natural intelligence. In addition, most of these characters, though unlearned, are highly competent talkers and storytellers. One need only examine the stage directions for any of Price's plays to see his concern and irritation with how rural southerners tend to be depicted: "[*Early Dark*] occurs in Warren County in northeastern North Carolina; but while that scene has shaped the people, it has not deformed them; and its characteristics should not be exploited for quaintness or humor, color or patronage. Such people could tell Sophocles or Beckett numerous complicated facts and possibilities."[29] Though Price sometimes displays an excessive fondness for his characters and their ways of living, he does not transform them into saints and common-man heroes. Rather, as Clayton Eichelberger points out, Price's characters "one after the other . . . fall short of realizing their potential" and "disappoint us finally by their failure to become what they are capable of being."[30] Weakness, often fueled by the temptations of alcohol and flesh, continually handicaps Price's characters—who are marvelous to listen to but quite often difficult to live with.

For nearly every Price character, family is the crucial factor in individual identity; as Price affirms, "[my novels] are very drenched in family."[31] In *Kate Vaiden* Kate's life is shaped by the murder-suicide of her parents, and in *The Surface of Earth* nearly every major character is affected monumentally by parents and grandparents. Whether blessing or curse, family is what influences, nourishes, stifles, and sometimes destroys a character's life. The most gripping and meaningful bonds for Price's characters are familial rather than matrimonial: father-son, father-daughter, son-mother, aunt- nephew. Comfort, nurture, and love are the primary exchange of such bonds, yet the bonds can often become oppressive and damaging. As Price states, family is "unquestionably the most destructive force there is, except for tornadoes."[32] Though not a determinist, Price demonstrates how family—which encompasses more than just living blood relations but includes one's genetic heritage—can be a virtually inescapable presence in one's life, as awesome as fate.

What makes Price's consideration of family particularly memorable is the way in which he reveals the role of sexuality in familial relations. According to Price, there is "an innate bi- or polysexuality in all creatures"; however, because "our forebears thought it a crucial condition for the maintenance of a perilous balance of power in family-centered societies," we are "now faced with a population unnaturally deprived of its most benign instincts."[33] Price believes humans have become blind to the "goodness of intimacy" between parents and children because any degree of intimacy is quickly transformed into anxiety and obsession with incest. Price's work reveals his belief that there are indeed sexual feelings between parents and children, yet he resists the common tendency to turn such feelings into sensationalized incestuous relations. Price instead strives to normalize family eroticism, place it within a more natural framework, while simultaneously demonstrating that real dangers and problems will arise if such intimacy goes too far.

If one were limited to a single word to describe the natural core of Price's writing, the most appropriate might be one of his own favorites: *mystery*. As Wallace Kaufman explains, "Price

UNDERSTANDING REYNOLDS PRICE

believes an author should pull us towards something. . . . some mystery. It should never be expected that the mystery will unveil itself and that, underneath, there'll be some clear, definite purpose. It is the artist's job to make us recognize and to show that, beneath the outer surfaces of life, there is some mystery."[34] Price himself adds that his objective is the "comprehension, control and celebration of the urgent mysteries" of the world.[35] Certainly the stories which have most interested Price are the biblical "mysteries," particularly the ones in which God makes his presence known to humans through either incarnation (the story of Jesus), words and deeds (Abraham and Isaac), or angelic messengers. Likewise has Price worked his own stories around human, spiritual, and supernatural mysteries: the appearance of ghosts in *A Generous Man, Love and Work,* and *The Source of Light;* the experience of visions in "The Names and Faces of Heroes" and *A Whole New Life;* literal or figurative metamorphoses in "The Enormous Door" and *The Tongues of Angels;* the transmission of external knowledge and warnings through dreams in *The Surface of Earth* and *Good Hearts;* and the appearance of angels and strange coincidences in numerous stories and novels.

Considering that Price is primarily a realist, these elements seem unusual, perhaps out of place. Does Price truly believe in ghosts and angels, and isn't their presence likely to alienate many readers? In an interview Price has said, "I do strongly suspect, even avow the existence and presence of forms of reality quite beyond those forms which we encounter in our daily routines," and he has added in a later interview, "we are limited as human beings by the capacities of our sense organs. There could be incredible visual phenomena actually occurring in this room right now which you and I simply can't see—no doubt they *are* occurring—because our retinas are only capable of responding to a very short portion of the spectrum of light. The room could be filled with angels, you know, dancing nude—and we wouldn't know it."[36] Though Price does not speak of personal encounters with ghosts, he displays an openness toward a world beyond the natural. Such an openness, though perhaps unusual in postmodern American fiction, is a common element of canonical literature (the Bible, Homer, Shakespeare, Milton) and even the pre-twentieth-century novel (Hawthorne, Melville, Dickens, the Brontës). As Price points out, "the problem with the twentieth century" is "the Loss of Faith"; many serious writers no longer seem curious about or entertain a belief in spiritual or supernatural occurrence.[37]

Though literary precedent may not entirely validate Price's use of supernaturalism, one finds in his work a useful lesson: that contemporary rationalism and skepticism have blinded individuals to the possibility of a world beyond the material. Price's work is centrally concerned with seeing, and those who look carefully and penetrate surface appearances may be rewarded with spiritual messages. Like the transcendentalists, Price believes that the self, the world, and God can be better understood through careful witness of nature, and that a spiritual world exists beyond or beneath the physical. Yet Price is more Christian mystic than transcendentalist, and even "mysticism" makes him somewhat uncomfortable because of its association with "the occult, or anything especially spooky or weird."[38] Instead Price attaches himself to mysticism as the term is defined in a "classical theological sense": a moment of "religious experience . . .

directly between a given creature and what he perceives to be the Creator."[39]

In his memoir *Clear Pictures,* Price describes an early mystical experience which he had as a child of six while roaming through the woods one afternoon: "I wedged my hunting knife into the soft bark of a pine tree. I pressed my lips to the dull edge of the cool blade. In that moment as I felt the tree's life in the steel, I knew that the world beyond me—every separate thing that was not Reynolds Price—was as alive as I. Through means that, then or now, I couldn't begin to explain, I knew that all matter was alive and aware—listening, seeing, hearing or feeling in its own way."[40] Such an experience sheds light on the relationship between humans and nature in much of Price's work: the natural landscape (animals, trees, rocks, plant life) is very much alive and offers messages for those humans attentive enough to receive them. For instance, in *The Tongues of Angels,* Bridge Boatner contends that "most of the urgent outstanding secrets of this one universe are strewn here before us. They are barely encoded, in faces and things, and are patiently waiting for the witness that will solve them."[41] Perhaps the most pressing message in all of Price's work is *watch the world carefully, be attentive to its messages.*

Unlike many contemporary writers who have described or viewed the world in terms of chaos and disorder, Price believes in a sense of design. He explains how his own adolescent reading of Tolstoy's *Anna Karenina* and Flaubert's *Madame Bovary* "deepened my sense of the complicity of all creation in some sort of joint enterprise, the sense of the boat that we're all in—from the amoebas and the AIDS viruses on up to brilliant nuclear scientists and the asteroids in outer space—they are all linked in some sort of design, I'm absolutely convinced. I've no sense at all that I know what that design is."[42] Nowhere is this design more visible than in *Good Hearts,* in which Price reveals how Providence operates in human affairs. When Wesley Beavers abandons his wife Rosa (Rosacoke Mustian, who is now Rosa Beavers), the events that follow—the arrival of her rapist, Wesley's eventual return from Nashville—suggest the hand of an unseen creator working a brand of inscrutable and complex justice. Though Price's use of Providence, along with his more general Christian faith, may alienate some contemporary readers, Price reminds one when he affirms the Apostles Creed that "virtually identical beliefs powered perhaps a majority of the supreme creative minds of our civilization—Augustine, Dante, Chaucer, Michelangelo, Dürer, Milton, Rembrandt, . . . Haydn, Mozart, Wordsworth, Beethoven, . . . Auden, O'Connor."[43]

For Price the novel has a high purpose and is not simply a verbal puzzle, a sociological treatise, or a political instrument. Instead the novel should reach to a deeper emotional and spiritual core, where it can respond to crucial questions and mysteries involving human affairs and human awareness of, perhaps even contact with, something greater—the presence of some creator. For Price there is a direct relationship between story and the human need for a godly presence; as he explains in *A Palpable God,* "The root of story sprang from need. . . . The need . . . for credible news that our lives proceed in order toward a pattern which, if tragic here and now, is ultimately pleasing in the mind of a god."[44] Though Price is attempting to lead readers to a spiritual understanding of the world, he is not forcibly didactic, proselytizing, or smug in his religious belief. His purpose—

beyond making readers aware of human, supernatural, and divine possibilities—is "to elicit understanding of and mercy toward as much creation [as] I can present, and you, the reader, can manage."[45] As Price states, "The end of fiction is mercy. . . . The whole point of learning about the human race presumably is to give it mercy."[46] Though perhaps not as fashionable or as easily accessible as certain other writers of his generation, Price offers a vision which is singular and bold.

CHAPTER TWO

The Mustian Novels

The Mustian family dominates Price's early work, figuring centrally in his first major fiction publication, a short story entitled "A Chain of Love" (1958), and in his first two novels, *A Long and Happy Life* (1962) and *A Generous Man* (1966). Though Price's cast of characters changed considerably and expanded after the mid-1960s, he returns periodically to the Mustians. In 1977 he published a dramatic version of *A Long and Happy Life* entitled *Early Dark,* which offers a slightly different rendering of the courtship of Rosacoke Mustian and Wesley Beavers;[1] and in 1988 he published *Good Hearts,* a novel which finds Rosacoke and Wesley nearly thirty years later. Though the short story is one of Price's finest and the play a moderate success, the focus in this chapter is on the three Mustian novels.

The Mustians are probably the least autobiographical figures in Price's fiction, though they may well be his most successful and fully realized characters. Rosacoke, Milo, Rato, and Emma Mustian, along with Wesley Beavers, are as memorable as any figures in Price's work. Rosacoke, in fact, though hardly Price's most interesting or unusual creation, may still be the character that readers best remember and most often associate with the author: she is perhaps to Price what Emma Bovary is to Flaubert or Anna Karenina to Tolstoy. Unlike those nineteenth-century heroines, though, Rosacoke does not commit adultery, living instead a fairly typical and relatively unadventurous life. The craft and achievement of Price's work is that he can make a

THE MUSTIAN NOVELS

country girl whose life never becomes particularly scandalous, much less unusual, worth watching. Whereas other southern writers such as Faulkner, Flannery O'Connor, and Carson McCullers are likely to offer grotesques and eccentric figures, Price is more attached to lives which appear, at least on the surface, relatively typical.

In contrast to Price's own mostly middle-class upbringing in small towns, the Mustians are a rural family of farmers, lower class socially and economically, with little formal education. Though Price writes in *Clear Pictures* of how he knew and observed people like the Mustians during his adolescence, his contact with them was minimal: "none of ['my country friends'] ever asked me to visit. So I never entered one of their houses."[2] How then did such a family come to dominate Price's work for a decade?

One explanation already mentioned is that during a rather difficult adolescence, in which the precocious and artistically inclined Price was tormented by several bullyish town children, the rural adolescents provided a haven. By turning to them in his fiction, Price not only offers his gratitude, but he finds a cast and setting for his stories which allow him to avoid being directly personal or autobiographical—something which Price was not ready to attempt at the time. In addition, the rural adolescents that Price knew revealed to him a much different world from the one with which he was familiar: "The world of piano lessons, neighborhood team-sports, clothing fads and the rest of that crowded American arcade of children's amusement . . . was as distant from their minds as the chance of careers in law, medicine or investment banking."[3]

UNDERSTANDING REYNOLDS PRICE

Each of Price's three Mustian novels—*A Long and Happy Life, A Generous Man,* and *Good Hearts*—follows a pattern in which a central character, confronted with a building pressure or change in life which is sexual in nature, is driven to some form of action to relieve that pressure. The action most often leads to a series of conflicts wherein the central character discovers the impossibility of his or her desires and is forced to settle upon some means of resolve which is not entirely satisfactory. In *A Long and Happy Life* Rosacoke Mustian finds herself unsettled by her desire for Wesley Beavers, and without feasible alternatives, she finally yields herself physically to him. Though the novel's conclusion offers the hope of resolution and acceptance, it is not necessarily the kind for which Rosacoke had hoped. In *A Generous Man* Milo Mustian has suddenly emerged into manhood, which brings rewards and confidence but also responsibility and questions concerning how he will utilize his gift, this newly discovered sexual energy. In Milo's case, resolution comes in the form of sad, even tragic, resignation. Finally in *Good Hearts* Wesley Beavers experiences pressure from a hungry libido which has gone unsatisfied in his marriage. Abandoning his wife, Rosa (née Rosacoke Mustian), Wesley moves in with a younger woman, but ultimately a series of events leads him to reconcile, however uncertainly, with his wife. Though the original turmoil is for the most part relieved by the end of each novel, the rest which the central characters earn is not always satisfying.

In addition to this familiar pattern, Price utilizes similar themes and tropes in each of the three novels. For instance, the conflict between family responsibility and freedom is powerful in each, as is the all-important gesture of gift-giving. Each of the three novels also deals with a significant ritual or moment of transformation: *A Long and Happy Life* offers an examination of courtship; *A Generous Man* looks at the crossing of a threshold, the emergence into manhood (perhaps *the* central ritual in Price's work); and *Good Hearts* concerns itself with separation in a long-established marriage. Price takes the Mustian family from adolescence into late middle-age, demonstrating how one family passes through and endures the various stages of life.

One aspect of the Mustian novels which is of particular interest and originality involves gender. Like Tolstoy, Flaubert, and James, Price demonstrates his ability to work across gender lines and create a believable and magnificent heroine—Rosacoke Mustian. As critics have pointed out, Price is highly skilled and competent when it comes to creating the voice, thoughts, and gestures of women; indeed, his most memorable creations are often female: Rosacoke, Kate Vaiden, Eva Mayfield. Yet in spite of, or perhaps in tandem with, this ability and ease in crossing gender lines, Price seems far more interested, at least in his Mustian novels, in male sexuality and beauty. The central erotic figure in each Mustian novel is a desirable, handsome, and virile male (Wesley Beavers, Milo Mustian), who attracts the gaze of women and men alike. Constance Rooke refers to such men in Price's work as "buccaneers."[4]

In these novels as in most of Price's work, male sexuality is not only celebrated, but it becomes the driving force behind the narrative: Wesley's erotic presence is what attracts Rosacoke and fuels her desire in *A Long and Happy Life;* Milo's newly realized erotic potential in *A Generous Man* endows him with a confidence and energy which attracts both women and men; and in *Good Hearts* Wesley's eroticism and good looks, which have made him "the kind of man people watch," compel him to leave his wife and take to the road. Whereas, historically speaking, it is more typical in novels concerned with love, marriage, and adultery to see a woman's body as a central figure of observation and desire, Price works against that tradition, placing the male body at the center and having women and men alike look on with awe, admiration, and desire. Though Price has resisted defining himself and his characters according to sexual categories—be it homo- , bi- , or heterosexuality—one certainly sees in his more autobiographical poetry, numerous depictions of homosexual love.

A Long and Happy Life

In order to understand fully the arrival of Reynolds Price's first novel in 1962, one should examine the original dust jacket. Though one indeed expects encomiums, Price's retinue of admirers there is unusually distinguished—Eudora Welty, Stephen Spender, Harper Lee, Lord David Cecil—and the praise itself is extended and extraordinary.[5] An unknown and relatively unpublished American writer, Reynolds Price, is compared to Joyce and Hemingway and is heralded for his "astonishing gifts" and "genius"; Lee predicts for him "a long and distinguished life in American letters." Though most reviewers and critics would later agree with this prepublication chorus of distinguished British and southern writers, others, such as Whitney Balliett of the *New Yorker,* would voice a strong dissent. In one of the rare negative reviews of the novel, Balliett wrote of how "the hot encomiums that cover the book's dust jacket . . . sound . . . so silly."[6] The prepublication endorsements for *A Long and Happy Life* contributed to the novel's success but conversely created a difficult critical environment for Price's future work. The expectations for such work would now be unusually high, and for some critics, Price would never be able to match the artistic success of his first novel. In addition, certain critics would never be comfortable with the speed and the process by which Price ascended as a writer.

Perhaps the most startling feature of *A Long and Happy Life,* and the one responsible for any comparison to Faulkner, is the opening sentence, which is two-thirds of a page in length, 192 words long. Balliett called it "garble," "written in imitation Faulkner—a wearisome and hopeless style," and *Time* magazine, though less critical, agreed it was an "opening bow toward Faulkner."[7] If Price was trying to establish his own literary identity, why write a sentence that would lead critics to press a comparison? One possibility is that even in this opening sentence Price does *not* sound like Faulkner. Jay Tolson takes this approach, arguing that although the sentence "looks as though it crawled straight out of Yoknapatawpha County," the prose is "for the most part, closely pruned, quite unlike Faulkner's sprawling verbal undergrowth." Tolson goes on to argue that the "other hallmarks of the Faulkner style" are missing, such as "the incantatory iterations, the neologisms, the poetic inflation."[8] For Tolson, as for an increasing number of critics, Faulkner's influence upon Price is insignificant, and any correlation between their work stems from the fact they are both southerners who are drawn to long sentences and rural settings.

A second possibility, offered by Michael Kreyling, is that Price does sound like Faulkner and for a good reason. Kreyling argues that Price, like a newly arrived figure skater, must "demonstrat[e] at the outset his own command of the compulsory figures. . . . Price's gambit in *A Long and Happy Life* seems an elegant turn: 'All right, audience, I can do a Triple-Faulkner without hitting the ice. Can we now get on with *my* novel?'"[9] The arguments of both Kreyling and Tolson are persuasive, though Kreyling's stance is weakened somewhat by Price's claim that "If I'd thought the sentence was Faulknerian, I'd never have published it. What it seems to me, all these years later, is a youthful and cocky rhetorical self-introduction, though it didn't (at the time) seem to me at all self-consciously extravagant."[10] Whether or not the sentence is in any way a bow to Faulkner, one realizes by the end of the novel that the vision of the two writers could not be any more different.

As for the sentence itself, it is such a beautiful and richly loaded beginning—Rooke refers to it as "a clarion call announcing the start of an important career"—that it warrants examination.[11] On the most primary level, Wesley Beavers is simply giving Rosacoke Mustian a ride on his motorcycle; however, the paragraph tells much more than that, as it both defines and prefigures the status of their relationship. Wesley, the essence of physical strength and grace, is driving this couple, but the ride and relationship is anything but smooth. "Switching coon tails in everybody's face," Wesley is fast, aggressive, and snake-like in his movements, and Rosacoke, "laid against his back like sleep," is simply holding on "for dear life." Price has created the perfect metaphor, in which the ride is the relationship. Going out with

Wesley is like riding on the back of his motorcycle; the course of movement is uncertain, dangerous, and fast, and one simply tries to hold on. The sentence itself, through its length, interruptions, shifts, and bumps, imitates the motorcycle ride, the literal breathlessness of it. In trying to hold on to meaning through the many movements and shifts in the sentence, the reader finds himself in the same position as Rosacoke, who is also trying to hold on, both figuratively and literally, to Wesley. Finally the sentence, with its sexually charged language, foreshadows and offers a rehearsal for the future "ride" the two will share in the broomstraw field. In this scene, like the later one, Wesley is the more active and physically aggressive force; Rosacoke, who is simply holding on, is the one acted upon: "spraddle-legged," "laid against his back," "her hands on his hips," "her white blouse blown out behind her like a banner in defeat," saying "Don't."

One could also argue that the sentence holds other clues as to the future of Wesley and Rosacoke. Though Wesley is steering the motorcycle, Rosacoke has determined their destination, the church at Mount Moriah, which seems fitting since Rosacoke's unstated objective throughout the novel is to get Wesley to a church to marry him. The irony, of course, is that at the end, when she finally has Wesley at a church with the promise of marriage, she is hardly satisfied. Perhaps Moriah, the place of Isaac's near-sacrifice by his loving father, Abraham, is significant. Rosacoke too will have to offer a sacrifice, ceding a part of herself and her ideals in order to be with Wesley.

A Long and Happy Life describes and explores a mating ritual, a courtship, in which two people at varying times and in divergent ways, pursue, retreat, prance about, test, and offer coded messages to one another, continually waiting to see how the other reacts. In a novel potent with rituals (a Christmas pageant, a birth, two funerals, a church picnic), the mating ritual is particularly crucial since it leads to the creation of families and thus to the continuance of life. As much as any American writer before him, Price has been centrally concerned with the family and the complex network of pressures, desires, and duties it imposes, and in his first novel he reveals this concern through his exploration not only of the Mustians but of a ritual which will lead to the formation of a new family.

In this particular mating ritual, which revolves around the question of what Wesley's intentions toward Rosacoke are, she plays the verbal aggressor, continually challenging the silent Wesley to voice those intentions. Elusive and enigmatic, Wesley resists Rosacoke's verbal challenges though he assumes the more aggressive role when it comes to pressing the physical bounds of their relationship. Each in his or her own way is pressing and testing the other, watching for a reaction and gauging whether tolerable communication (verbal and physical) is possible. Through their letters, dialogue, and physical contact (on the motorcycle, in the broomstraw field), Rosacoke and Wesley attempt to fit together in a mutually satisfactory manner.

Their mating ritual, of course, changes dramatically after their sexual encounter. Up to that point Rosacoke has been the driving force, shepherding them across difficult terrain while Wesley remained elusive. After their meeting in the field, they switch roles. Rosacoke becomes slightly mysterious and resistant, and Wesley, as if to take up the slack, becomes the more primary force drawing them together. The key to this shift in balance involves the offering of a gift. Rosacoke has given herself and her body to Wesley, yet he has not accepted her in the proper manner. As Price writes in his notebook for this novel, Rosacoke's "greatness as a woman" lies with "her desire, her obligation, always to make the kind gesture, the touch, the thing which seemed to her clearly, if not always desirably, *right,* and right because she thought it would make somebody else happy."[12]

Gift giving is at the heart of *A Long and Happy Life:* nature continually is bestowing gifts, children are viewed as gifts, the community is searching for the proper Christmas gift for Mr. Isaac, Rato brings a sackful of gifts from Oklahoma, the Wise Men bring gifts to the baby Jesus during the pageant. Rosacoke, too, strives to bestow the appropriate gift whether it be stockings for Mildred Sutton or her own body for Wesley Beavers. Yet her gifts mostly misfire. She arrives with the stockings to find Mildred dead, and Wesley calls her "Mae" and shines a flashlight into the sky immediately after she has given herself to him. Price writes that when gifts go unacknowledged or are not properly received, "the important thing is knowing what to do then, knowing how . . . to 'connect.'"[13] This is precisely Rosacoke's dilemma at the end of the novel when she tells herself "that it is very lonely, donating things to people that they don't need or even want."[14] She is wrong about Wesley's not needing or wanting her, though she is correct in realizing that her gift has not been fully appreciated. Fittingly, the couple is brought together at the end by the offering once again of a gift, their unborn child; and though they in no way desired or sought such a gift, it nevertheless promises them a future together, whether blissful or tragic, and thus ends the mating ritual.

The term *mating ritual,* suggestive of animals and nature, applies rather well to one of the more brilliant features of *A Long and Happy Life:* the way in which Price integrates his young lovers into a pastoral setting, presenting them as creatures in harmony with nature. Most of the novel takes place outdoors, and the landscape—as seen in the spring, woods, trees, animals, dust, pine needles, and rocks—is familiar and alive. Within this natural setting many of the major events in the characters' lives take place: Rosacoke's first sighting of Wesley in Mr. Isaac's pecan tree; Rosacoke and Mildred's sighting of the deer in the broomstraw field; Rosacoke and Wesley's sexual encounter in a similar field. Nature is a character in the novel, a living presence, and for those who watch carefully, it offers signs and messages.

A Long and Happy Life operates within the pastoral tradition, and Price's reference in his notebook to Longus's third-century pastoral romance "Daphnis and Chloe" (as offering a model for dealing with the presentation of a sexual scene), indicates that Longus's story may have played an even greater role in Price's creation of a modern pastoral. Like "Daphnis and Chloe," *A Long and Happy Life* focuses on the courtship of two young rustic lovers living in an enclosed Arcadia, working their love toward a final consummation. As with Longus's romance, Price's narrative pays particular attention to the male body as it is observed with awe and desire by the female, and one of the more memorable scenes in *A Long and Happy Life*—in which Rosacoke observes and is drawn to Wesley as he plays a harmonica on the porch—mirrors a similar scene in the earlier romance in which Chloe watches the beautiful Daphnis playing on his pipe.

Price's use of the pastoral emphasizes a harmony between man and animal, and man and nature. For instance, Wesley, whose last name is "Beavers" and who is first seen making snake-like movements and "switching coon tails," is likened to a large, strong bird of prey, an eagle in a tree, a hawk sailing overhead; on other occasions he is seen as a cardinal, a snake, a deer, a fish, and a hornet. In addition, as Rooke points out, Wesley is "identified with the natural force of water": he is "this ex-Navy man who skinny-dips at Ocean View, who swims and dives so beautifully at Mason's spring-fed lake."[15] Wesley is a creature of nature, a natural man, responding to the same impulses and stimuli that affect other animals: hunger, sexuality, recognition of danger. And though Rosacoke is not endowed with these myriad animal metaphors and similes, she too is a creature of nature. Whether or not she realizes it, her attraction to Wesley, which has dominated her thoughts for eight years, is largely physical and sexual in nature.

In its examination and description of a mating ritual, the novel is concerned with the decisions and sacrifices facing Rosacoke and Wesley. For Rosacoke, courtship leads to childbirth and children, and few novels are more loaded with pregnant women, screaming babies, and mothers as well as babies dying during the ordeal of birth. In a novel which begins with the funeral of a woman who has died in childbirth, and ends with the welcoming of a baby into the world (Jesus, and also Rosacoke's unborn child), Price emphasizes the double-edged nature of bearing a child: the joy and delight, yet the pain and possibility of death. The danger of birth is a continual presence in the novel: Mildred Sutton and Horatio Mustian III both die as a result of the trauma it inflicts, and childbirth is even associated tangentially with the death of Rosacoke's father, who dies while his wife is pregnant.

At the center of this swirl of activity involving babies and pregnancies is Rosacoke, who is not only affected by these traumatic and tragic births but continually finds herself in the position of having to quiet a crying baby: Frederick Gupton at the church picnic, Sledge at Mary Sutton's house, and Frederick again at the Christmas pageant. Rosacoke's maternal skills and instincts are not particularly strong early on as she runs from the crying Sledge and fails to assist at Sissie's delivery. It is as if Rosacoke senses what is happening to her, that she is being trapped in the role of nurturer and mother by both her biology and the community (among other things, the novel is about Rosacoke's initiation into motherhood, how she is alerted to and prepared for its responsibilities). By the novel's conclusion, though, Rosacoke responds successfully to the crying Gupton baby, suggesting perhaps her secret acceptance not only of her pregnancy but of her new role. This final scene in one respect is celebratory, offering the anticipation of a new life, and light, which may guide Rosacoke and Wesley.

Is Price then forecasting "a long and happy life" for his young lovers? Certainly many of the early reviewers and readers saw it that way, though critics since have recognized the artfulness of Price's irresolution. Though it appears at the end of the novel that Rosacoke and Wesley will come together, marry, and raise this child, that does not necessarily mean happily ever after. Rosacoke has been successful in catching her man—the elusive

Wesley has offered marriage and a home—yet at what price? Her sexual encounter with Wesley has taught Rosacoke that life with him will not be what she imagined; it may include "eating Post Toasties" in a rented room, pressing shirts, and staring out a window at concrete roads.

There is an element of tragedy and resignation in this final pageant scene; as Price writes in his notebook, "[Rosacoke] suddenly realizes the tragedy of growing up: involvement and responsibility."[16] And there is certainly enough foreshadowing for us to imagine the worst about an impending marriage between Rosacoke and Wesley. The lines from "We Three Kings" which Wesley sings portend a dark future:

> Myrrh is mine, its bitter perfume
> Breathes a life of gathering gloom.
> Sorrowing, sighing, bleeding, dying,
> Sealed in the stone-cold tomb. (188)

Yet there are also encouraging signs. Rosacoke is able to calm the hungry and struggling male child on her lap, and her affirmative "yes" to both the child and her present condition suggests hope. In addition, the novel—which began with a breathless motor-cycle ride and then proceeded over the waves and troughs of Rosacoke's turmoil—ends with an image of rest. This final moment seems well-earned by Rosacoke and indicative of a more peaceful future. In fact, the novel ends with the word *love,* an encouraging sign that perhaps their love will endure.

One can also look to the epigraph for an indication of what the future may hold for Wesley and Rosacoke. Taken from Dante's *Paradiso,* the epigraph translates as:

> for I have seen, all winter through, the brier
> display itself as stiff and obstinate,
> and later, on its summit, bear the rose. . . .[17]

In this novel—which stretches from July to December and concerns itself with the cyclical nature of life (birth, marriage, pregnancy, death)—spring is promised, a time which will bring the rose to blossom. Certainly this portends well for Rosacoke, who in assuming the role of the Virgin during the pageant becomes the rose itself. Yet as Allen Shepherd points out, the lines following the ones which Price quotes (and Price uses ellipses, perhaps to prompt one to read further in Dante) show a ship, after a long voyage, finally reaching the mouth of a harbor, where it promptly sinks, suggesting that one "should not be deceived by false appearances or come to hasty conclusions."[18] Rosacoke and Wesley may bloom like the rose, or sink like the ship. The beauty and art of Price's ending is its crafted ambiguity, in which elements of celebration, rest, tragedy, and disappointment commingle, striking a most human chord.

A Generous Man

Though *A Generous Man* (1966), Price's second novel, returns to the Mustian family and the rural North Carolina setting of *A Long and Happy Life,* it is not a sequel, and though it is set nine years prior in 1948, not truly a prequel. For the most part *A Generous Man* is an independent story with little narrative or thematic connection to the earlier novel; in other words, the second novel does not expand upon the first, except to surprise and perhaps sadden the reader with the knowledge that Milo Mustian of *A Long and Happy Life* has apparently wasted the great potential he once possessed.

Whereas the earlier novel focuses on Rosacoke Mustian and her troubled love for Wesley Beavers, *A Generous Man* is Milo's story; and whereas the earlier novel is tightly controlled and primarily realistic, *A Generous Man* is looser in construction and more farcical and absurd in nature. There is little question as to which of the two is the better novel—*A Long and Happy Life* is flawlessly constructed and more emotionally engaging—yet in spite of its excesses, *A Generous Man* takes more risks and perhaps offers more rewards upon multiple readings.

For the most part *A Generous Man* received positive reviews—an accomplishment, considering that as a second novel following the tremendous success of Price's first, it was the object of high expectation. Yet as a more elusive and unusual novel, *A Generous Man* also confused readers—indeed, confused them to such a degree that Price was later compelled to write an explanatory essay, "News for the Mineshaft: An Afterword to *A Generous Man,*" with the purpose of "correct[ing] a few misunderstandings."[19]

The primary point of confusion concerns the work's genre. With its contrived plot, numerous coincidences, prophecies, ghosts, and absurd situations, *A Generous Man* departs from conventions of the realistic novel. Though the jacket cover calls it a novel, Price writes in his essay that "*A Generous Man* is not a novel"; instead he likens it to the late plays of Shakespeare, Japanese Noh drama, and Mozart's *The Magic Flute,* in that it "negotiate[s] with . . . a real world which is capable of swelling at moments of intensity to a mysterious, transfigured world, a world in which all manner of 'unrealistic' events can and will occur—the return of the dead, outrageous coincidence, great rushes of communication between people, great avowals of love or hate."[20] The term *romance,* which typically allows for improbability and freedom from restrictions of verisimilitude, would be appropriate were it not for the ending; as Price himself writes, "surely the minimal requirement for romance is a happy ending," which *A Generous Man* does not have.[21] Because the text darkens in part three, concluding on a grim and perhaps tragic note, *romance* is not quite appropriate. Price himself has suggested the terms *tragic romance* and *sad pastoral,* and Daniel Frederick Daniel speaks of the text as a "fantasy" in the Tolkien sense.[22] Since discussions about genre, particularly in regard to problematic texts, have a way of going on ad infinitum, it seems expedient to say that any of these terms can be used, even *novel* in the broad generic sense, so long as one realizes *A Generous Man* does not operate like other realistic narratives.

Related to this question of genre is one of license and accountability. Though Price has asked readers not to judge *A Generous Man* as if it were a conventional, realistic novel, does that give him free rein to contrive the plot, send in a ghost, put uncharacteristic words into a fifteen-year-old's mouth, and justify it simply by saying, I'm not writing a novel, I'm writing a romance, or something that's like a romance, a contemporary *Winter's Tale* or *Tempest*? One wonders about accountability here, and whether the writer is simply making an excuse for a novel which did not work. The only way to know is by asking another question, which will be answered later in this chapter:

does the end justify the means? The introduction of a ghost, for instance, need not sabotage or compromise a text, as one sees in the work of Shakespeare, Ibsen, Henry James, and the Brontës, yet there must be some just explanation for the presence of such nonrealistic elements.

The plot of *A Generous Man,* which is dependent upon long passages of exposition, is one of Price's most complex. Milo Mustian awakens on a Saturday morning in October of 1948 following his apparent sexual initiation of the night before with a young traveling carnival girl named Lois Provo.[23] On this particular morning Milo, who is on the verge of becoming the man in the family (his father is dead, his grandfather is aging), accompanies his family to the veterinarian's in Warrenton because his brother Rato's dog, Phillip, is ill. The dog, who might be mad, gets loose and rouses a giant python named Death from the county fair, and both animals escape into the woods; the snake is owned by Lois's aunt, Selma Provo, who one later learns is actually Lois's mother. Rato goes in search of Phillip, and the men of the town, led by Sheriff Rooster Pomeroy, form a posse to find Rato, Phillip, and the snake; they are in effect hunting Death. During the course of the hunt, Milo gets drunk and sleeps with the sheriff's wife, Kate Pomeroy, who years before had loved a boy who resembles Milo and was in fact Milo's relative. That same boy, whose name was Tommy Ryden, is coincidentally Selma's former lover and thus the father of Lois. Though dead, Tommy continues to walk the earth as a ghost, and on a country road he and Milo encounter one another. The meeting is strange and ends with the ghost's not only striking Milo but leading him to the missing insurance money, which will now go to Lois. Ultimately, the python is killed before it can kill Milo, the truth of Lois's identity is revealed, and Rato and Milo return home safely. All of this occurs in the course of about forty-eight hours, between Saturday morning and Monday morning.

Though the plot of *A Generous Man* is outrageous and Dickensian, and thus atypical of Price's work, the novel's subject, a young man's emergence into manhood, is familiar as are its themes: loss and wasted opportunity, identity, freedom versus responsibility, gift-giving and debt-paying, how the supernatural operates through the natural. Perhaps no other single moment in the course of a human life interests Price more than the male's arrival at the threshold of manhood—the moment in which he becomes both a sexual creature, full of need, desire and gratitude, and an adult, capable of making choices and discovering freedom.[24] Many of Price's best short stories ("The Enormous Door," "Deeds of Light," "His Final Mother"), along with several of his novels (*A Generous Man, The Surface of Earth, The Tongues of Angels*), focus upon adolescent boys who are either approaching or passing into manhood. In some cases the boy is fatherless (Milo, Rob in *Surface,* Marcus Black in "Deeds"), and thus the rise into manhood takes on added significance: the boy is becoming the head of the household.

The most crucial aspect of the boy's emergence, particularly in Milo's case, involves recognition of one's sexuality. Milo's sudden awareness of his sexual powers overshadows everything else in his life and signals his tremendous potential. Yet for Milo and several of Price's other protagonists, the future becomes disappointing, even tragic, because these young men cannot

sustain their sexual energy, settling instead for a life of conformity and rest.

A Generous Man actually begins with Milo's arrival or birth
into manhood. He is first seen naked and in bed, dreaming about
his sexual initiation of the night before, while his mother calls,
"Milo. Son?" (each of the three sections of the novel begins with
Milo's being awakened). The fact he is naked and suddenly
transformed suggests birth or rebirth: Milo is waking to a new
life. Overnight he has become a man, brimming with confidence
in his gifts and attractiveness.

His mother's opening question "Son?" is also significant as
it plays into the identity theme in the novel: who exactly is Milo?
Is he a man now? This, of course, relates to questions concerning
Milo's name. Though he claims to be named for a Greek wrestler,
a man of strength who was later eaten by wolves, the greater
likelihood is that he was named for either an ancestor or Papa's
"old blind mule." The question of Milo's identity—several
characters ask him quite literally, "Who are you?"—is crucial in
the novel, and it will be complicated by the presence of Tommy
Ryden, whose spirit seems to be working through Milo. In
addition, the question of identity extends to others in the novel,
particularly the animals. The snake, for instance, is variously
described as a python, a boa constrictor, "Death," and the spirit
of Tommy. And the identity of Phillip the dog, who appears to be
half terrier and half mystery (Rato said "Airedale" and Milo said
"Traveling salesman"), is in question. Even Selma, Lois's aunt,
is not who she appears to be. Price is questioning the stability of
identity and the appropriateness of names, while demonstrating
how others, particularly blood ancestors, work through and play

a role in determining the identity and fate of their descendants.

Certainly the primary force shaping and changing Milo's identity is his budding sexuality. He has, in essence, arrived; it is his day: "his mouth burst open on the surge of his joy, the sudden manhood that stood in his groin, that firmed the bones of his face and wrists as the truck bore him on through this clear day."[25] The phrase "clear day"—one of Price's working-titles for the novel until he learned of a new Broadway show entitled *On a Clear Day You Can See Forever,* which the papers were calling *Clear Day*—functions, along with related words such as "day," "morning," and "night," as a motif in the novel, indicating Milo's sexual potential.[26] Through his newly realized sexuality, Milo has acquired power and confidence, drawing others to him and offering hope for the community. As critics have pointed out, Price makes use of fertility plots and quest motifs in painting Milo as the young virile hero, the seed-bearer, the man possessing restorative powers.[27] He is the young knight on a quest, whose mission is to subdue the monster Death, rescue maidens in distress (Kate, Lois), and bring about a return to order and truth by finding Rato and restoring to Lois what is rightfully hers, the insurance money and her true identity.

Rooster Pomeroy, the sterile and impotent though spirited sheriff, plays the role of the comic guide and advises Milo to seize the day while he can: "Use what the good Lord give you *now,* and use it every chance the day provides. . . . Don't think it's morning when it's late afternoon" (86). Rooster even appears to contrive Milo's sexual encounter with his wife Kate, intended not only to bring Rooster a child but to cure his wife of the spell she has been under for thirteen years. Milo gives himself sexually to Kate (and it is more an act of giving than it ostensibly was with Lois), and by this point his energy and attractiveness have become so potent that there appears no end to what he can do both for himself and others. As the title indicates, Milo is a "generous man," a man who has much to give.

Milo's giving continues for most of the novel, particularly when he aids Tommy Ryden's spirit in making amends to Lois, but then suddenly his potential, his intensity, vanishes. Once the insurance money is restored to Lois, Milo becomes his old self: "for *Milo* he was again, only himself, a tired wounded boy, harmless, powerless, abandoned by Tom as finally as [Selma], with less of Tom now in his face and person than most cousins share" (241). The loss of Tom's spirit returns Milo to the ordinary world; as one sees in both *A Generous Man* and *A Long and Happy Life,* Milo will not leave home and become the world's "volunteer" for those in "serious need" of help. Instead he opts for his "old plan . . . to live on here and work like a mill from day to dark every day but Christmas" (267). Somewhat like Rosacoke in *A Long and Happy Life,* though to a far greater degree, Milo settles. As Clayton Eichelberger writes of Price's characters, "They win our affection only to disappoint us finally by their failure to become what they are capable of being; and we stand by like bound men, mute, helpless to reach out."[28]

Price himself says that the theme of *A Generous Man* is loss, "loss in the midst of plenty or at the sudden end of plenty."[29] Milo has much to offer, but he is unable to sustain the use of the gifts that he himself has been given, and so he loses them. This is a familiar occurrence in Price's oeuvre and in conventional society—the individual sacrificing his potential in order to avoid danger, vulnerability, and conflict. Like so many others, Milo returns to everyday reality, settling into a safer, less-conflicted life where he will become, in Price's words, "this rather raucous, burnt-out jokester . . . who disgusts even his sister."[30]

In answer to why Milo's young manhood is so different from the rest of his life, Price says, "So is the youth of most men."[31] Energetic individuals like Milo are unable to maintain their intensity in adulthood because, as Price says, "it gets them in trouble constantly"; thus they must "give up that energy as soon as society honorably permits them."[32] Though passage into manhood is a magical, exuberant time in Price's narratives, it can also signal the beginning of tragic resignation.

Price's own interpretation of the book's conclusion is that Milo's "life is essentially over; the *good* part of his life is essentially over."[33] Some may find solace in the fact that Milo's final word to Lois is "Morning," and that the novel's concluding sentence is an image of a clear and rather beautiful morning: "It was morning (clear, cloudless, the oldest gift), would be morning oh six hours yet" (275). However, Price explains, "the sense is heavy at the end . . . that it was his last day, that—in Donne's use of the same metaphor—'His first minute, after noon, is night.' The final light of the book is still morning, but morning for only 'six hours yet.'"[34] For those who persist in reading a happy ending, or ponder what Milo might have done had he left home, Price adds: "The boy is quite unequipped to pursue the sort of knight-errantry that he seems to have in mind, that he seems to feel is required by the situation of the world."[35]

As a novel about Milo's newly realized manhood, and his subsequent refusal to seek the fruits of that manhood, the work leads one to question the presence of the nonrealistic elements within it: the appearance of a ghost; the precocity of Milo's words and thoughts; the excessive coincidences involving Tommy, Kate, Lois, and Selma; the absurd nature of the hunt. Because most of these elements stretch the credibility of the story, they prompt us to wonder why they are here and what they add. An initial response, perhaps the most basic, is that they entertain. A ghost who assists in changing a flat tire, a snake named Death who is being hunted by an inept posse, ten thousand dollars falling from an outhouse ceiling—each of these elements amuses and intrigues us. In this novel, more than any of his others, Price reveals his comic side.

A Generous Man is filled with comic dialogue, strange misunderstandings, and terrific word play and symbolic activity. For instance, consider how Price plays with the word *snake*. When Milo tells Rosa of his activities of the previous night, he speaks on more than one level, "[Lois and I] were taking that snake for a walk through the woods. . . . And we're exercising him again tonight, just her and me" (6). Later Rosacoke says of one of the Ryden boys, "I wouldn't even tell the things he does—to girls mainly, putting things on them. Snakes—slimy!" (55). The phallic jokes continue, though they do not necessarily seem forced or even conscious on the writer's part: one learns that the snake is enormous (eighteen feet long), that it does not have a face, that it is harmful and hungry, that it is dangerous when loose, and that it goes by the name of Death. In addition, it seems playfully appropriate that the spirit of the phallic Tommy Ryden resides in the form of a snake and that the posse, led by an impotent sheriff, is trying to find that same snake, which is owned by a woman who is hysterical over having lost it. Though some critics have not enjoyed the comic phallicism of the novel, Price has carried it off rather well, and much of the humor remains fresh nearly thirty years after the novel was written.

Beyond simple entertainment, though, the nonrealistic elements of the novel serve other purposes. For instance, the precocity of Milo's thoughts and actions help to emphasize his intense confidence and exuberance during this particular stage in his life. The swelling of Milo's world of possibilities is reflected in the swelling of his language. Though his words and acts are not realistic, they demonstrate the fullness of his sudden emergence into manhood. As for other nonrealistic elements, such as the comic handling of the hunt, Price explains that one purpose of the novel was "the guying of as many as possible of the sacred solemnities of Southern fiction," such as "the humble but noble dog, the pathetic idiot, the sanctity of blood and name . . . the hunters who think they are chasing bear or boar but end with nothing more edible than Beauty and Truth in their gassy bags, the young stud watering some parched lady's life."[36] Thus, the excesses of *A Generous Man* serve a satiric purpose.

The most outrageous nonrealistic element in the novel, which also provides the text's central mystery, is the character of Tommy Ryden's ghost. Many reviewers failed to mention the ghost, perhaps because Price presents him as being like any other human being, a portrayal Price supports through precedent: "What has interested me always about ghost stories—respectable, well-authenticated ghost stories—is that ghosts almost always appear in unexceptional corporeal form. That is, they do not appear as filmy, vaporous, emanations of light but have simply—and terribly—the opaque reality of a live person walking through a room or sitting in a chair." Price offers the possibility there may be forms of life and energy which return from beyond the grave. As he says, "there are a great many things in the universe which we don't understand but make constant use of—electricity, the energy of the atom. . . . I do strongly suspect, even avow the existence and presence of forms of reality quite beyond those forms which we encounter in our daily routines."[37]

The appearance of Tommy's spirit has a more significant function, though, than merely challenging the reader to consider the possibility that ghosts may exist. Through Tommy, Price demonstrates how the dead shape the lives of the living. For instance, the strong physical resemblance between Tommy and Milo leads those who once knew Tommy to see his spirit present in Milo. Price is suggesting an individual's dead ancestors can genetically work through that individual and help determine his fate. Milo has acquired Tommy's looks and magnetic appeal, though he will make rather different use of those gifts.

What is most fascinating and mysterious about the connection between Tommy and Milo is how Price reveals the dead figure to be an active force, rather than just a composite of passed-down traits. Milo not only acquires characteristics from Tommy but finds himself being utilized by Tommy's spirit. Tommy uses Milo as an agent through which he can work his will and repay old financial and emotional debts; because of these debts it appears that Tommy is being divinely punished, forced to wander like the Ancient Mariner and seek amends. Price's depiction of the dead man as an active and irresistible spirit, using and manipulating the living, is unique in contemporary American literature.

In psychological terms Tommy is Milo's double or doppelgänger, a mirror image of Milo who has lived the life Milo rejects at the end of the novel. Whereas Tommy opted for

freedom, Milo turns toward family responsibility and conformity, leading the reader to question whether Tommy's example
plays some role in Milo's decision at the end. Perhaps the
suffering of Tommy's spirit leads Milo to choose a more conser-
vative future. Whatever the case, the unusual relationship between Tommy and Milo breaks new ground in demonstrating that
the dead may play a far greater role in the lives of the living than
is commonly assumed.

Good Hearts

Price's decision to return after more than twenty-five years
to the familiar characters of an earlier novel—Wesley Beavers
and Rosacoke Mustian (now Rosa Beavers) of *A Long and Happy
Life*—is hardly unusual in contemporary American literature.
Updike returns every ten years to Rabbit Angstrom; Roth has
done the same with Nathan Zuckerman; and Heller has recently
resurrected *Catch-22*'s Yossarian. That Price waited so long is
not due to the fact that his readers were uninterested; as he has
affirmed on more than one occasion, they have continually been
curious as to the whereabouts of Rosacoke and Wesley. The
problem was that Price himself had dismissed the issue, at least
to the degree that he was not eager to write another novel about
them: "I'd occasionally wondered if her and her husband's
ongoing lives were interesting enough for another look; but I
always concluded they were sadly becalmed in normal existence."[38] The word *sadly* is conspicuous, suggesting that, for
Price, marriage leads to a calm resignation rendering individuals
uninteresting.

THE MUSTIAN NOVELS

Price's attitude toward Rosacoke and Wesley changed in the mid-1980s when his own life, threatened by cancer, changed dramatically: "I had some awareness that again I was plotting the course of lives parallel to mine—years of fairly smooth sailing in work and love, then shipwreck."[39] Certainly Price's experience with "the eel," the malignant tumor which fought for control of his body, parallels Rosa's violation by the rapist; in addition, the Beavers, like Price, were forced after a catastrophe to begin new lives.

Whereas *A Long and Happy Life* offers a close examination of a courtship and the beginning of a family, *Good Hearts* is Price's marriage novel, providing a careful look at that same marriage in mid- to late stream twenty-eight years later. For a writer whose central material is the family, Price has not been particularly optimistic about marriage. A lifelong bachelor, Price claims he has witnessed only a couple of marriages that he "envied," and there is a sense in his work that marriage, beyond being difficult and trying, is constrictive, somewhat unnatural, and potentially lethal.[40] Rosa, in fact, seems to function in *Good Hearts* as Price's sociological mouthpiece, arguing how America has created an atmosphere which pressures people into thinking "that life without a richly contented marital love-life is worse than being staked down to the jailhouse floor in a banana republic in the worst month of summer with roaches big as pancakes."[41] Marriage has become "so unrealistically important," says Rosa, and carries with it such high expectations, that failure seems inevitable.

Yet Jefferson Humphries, who refers to *Good Hearts* as Price's "most compelling and sensitive book," writes of the novel's tremendous utility in regard to marriage: "There cannot be a subject on which Americans of all ages living in 1988 more desperately need and crave . . . instruction: Can two good people live together for long without suffering or doing subtle, maybe invisible but nonetheless real, harm to themselves and each other . . . ?"[42] Though Price does not explicitly provide an answer, one would guess his response to be *Perhaps, but it's tremendously difficult.*

As for Price's depiction of marriage in *Good Hearts,* one sees a departure from the typical literature dealing with marriage, separation, and adultery. In this subgenre of literature, which includes such canonical works as *Anna Karenina* and *The Scarlet Letter,* one is likely to encounter drama, passion, perhaps even tragedy. In addition, one of the members of the central married couple is often depicted as embodying passion (Anna Karenina, Hester Prynne), while the other is a cold-blooded villain (Karenin, Chillingworth). In *Good Hearts* Price resists tragic passion, intense drama, and extreme characterizations, opting instead for characters who are compassionate, even- tempered, unselfish, and basically good. Price, in fact, goes out of his way to state that Rosa and Wesley possess *good hearts,* "as good as any you've met unless you meet more saints than most" (6). These are good people, with good jobs and a good home, who mostly do good things for one another—not the typical characters who make for good fiction. Yet somehow they do. Price demonstrates that after enough time, even good people are likely to harm one another, though the harm is hardly blatant or aggressive; it simply comes from their not being attentive enough to each other.

One can see how Price lays out the relationship between Rosa and Wesley in the novel's opening scene, which—though

THE MUSTIAN NOVELS

not as stunning or as artfully complex as the long beginning sentence of *A Long and Happy Life*—is nevertheless mysteriously intimate. Price begins by taking the reader inside Rosa and Wesley's bedroom, yet not for what one typically sees in contemporary literary bedroom scenes; instead Rosa and Wesley are readying for sleep. The routine of their marriage is apparent: they offer familiar end-of-the-day messages to one another ("I hope we both sleep safe"), feel an "ease in one another's nearness," and enter sleep on their backs as "always." In the hands of most writers this scene would settle into boredom or clichéd sentimentality, but Price keeps it mysterious by setting the scene on or near the darkest day of the year, casting the room in an eery light (Rosa and Wesley are viewed with "a glow on their skin like the shine of phosphorus on underwater life"), and allowing the reader the unique opportunity of viewing a couple's private nighttime ritual. By addressing the reader directly—"You though, if you'd been transparent there, would have seen . . ."—Price heightens the voyeuristic involvement: the reader is not only watching Rosa and Wesley in their bedroom but is aware of his own presence there as a voyeur, an intruder. Price will later and similarly describe the rapist Wave as a voyeur of Rosa and Wesley's lives, presenting a strange correspondence and identification between reader and rapist.

In addition, the fact that Rosa and Wesley are not having sex—some might call this the archetypal marriage scene—makes them somehow more vulnerable to the reader's penetrating and intrusive eyes than if Price had graphically described them in the throes of sexual union. One is witnessing what Price suggests is the secret shame and failure of marriage, "the benign neglect which permits two bodies so warm and fine to resist quick union" (4). *Benign neglect* is as important a term as any in understanding this marriage and thus this novel. Through their familiarity, Rosa and Wesley have stopped paying careful attention to one another; this neglect not only threatens their marriage but qualifies for Price as a human error bordering on sin or evil: they have failed to appreciate and utilize the gift of their bodies, and they have rejected their vows to one another. Further, by directly addressing and placing his reader in the Beavers' bedroom, Price is suggesting that his reader, the "you," is perhaps guilty of the same benign neglect.

A final point of interest in this opening scene concerns Price's use of dreams and the unconscious. Few writers devote as much attention to the sleeping and dreaming hours of their characters as Price, yet considering that such hours account for nearly a third of human life and generate some of the most mysterious and urgent moments, his attention seems warranted. Rosa's opening dream, in which she imagines herself reading a poem about Wesley to a roomful of people, is reassuring and speaks to her contentment with their marriage. Wesley's dream, however, in which he sees himself naked in a roomful of strangers, is unsettling and testifies to his sense of failure and discontent. As evident through their "clashing dreams," Rosa and Wesley are in a state of disharmony, yet they appear oblivious to the situation as they awaken from this "strange night" looking as "calm as children." Wesley, though, has received the message from his unconscious, and by the end of the scene, he leaves— severing their marriage. All of this occurs without a single moment of spoken conflict or conscious friction between them.

Though *Good Hearts* deals with the same characters as *A*

Long and Happy Life, it is a different kind of novel, revealing the evolution of Price's style and vision. For instance, his language has become simpler and closer to contemporary speech; as Monroe Spears explains, "there are no more long, dreamy sentences to evoke a pastoral world, no idyllic distancing."[43] Though a partial explanation for this change is that sections of the novel are delivered in Rosa's voice, which demands a simpler and more colloquial style of English, one finds that Price's voice and vision have indeed evolved. Whereas *A Long and Happy Life* is pastoral in nature, limning a world of rural isolation, *Good Hearts* is semi-urban, contemporary, and media- affected. The entire story of *A Long and Happy Life* is set within a small green circle of rural space, an Arcadia, into which the rest of America and the world do not ostensibly intrude. *Good Hearts,* though, takes place in middle-sized southern cities—Raleigh and Nashville—and Price's characters are now tuned in to that outside world of *PM Magazine, The Young and the Restless, People* magazine, Kenny Rogers, AIDS, and Fredrick's of Hollywood. This is a new strain in Price's writing, signaling a change not only in his vision but also in the lifestyle of individuals and communities of the upper South; the presence of television and mass communication has become so great it can no longer be ignored.

Price's use of television, the media, and pop culture differs dramatically from that of, say, Don DeLillo. Whereas DeLillo attempts to demonstrate how American behavior has been shaped by television, Price resists attributing such power and influence to that medium, insisting that a good many people continue to live and think for themselves despite heavy TV watching. Price's characters are not manipulated or excessively influenced by television; instead it functions as entertainment, a freak show providing laughs and misguided information. Though TV talk shows, news polls, and pop psychologies are continuously telling Americans how they should feel, Price demonstrates through Rosa how reductive and inaccurate these polls and programs are. Unlike the characters in DeLillo's *White Noise,* who react exactly as television directs them, Price's Rosa responds to her rape in a manner distinct from that prescribed by pop psychology: "All the reading I've done says that rape victims first go through a bad stage of hating their own bodies. . . . I didn't hate my body or anything about me" (38). Price presents Rosa and Wesley as wise rurals, whose more natural wisdom contrasts with and proves superior to that brand of collective thinking dominating the air waves.

Price's use of, and argument about, television and the mass media is refreshing, as he demonstrates that Rosa is not most women, that individuals are not statistics, and that pop psychology and television are hardly authorities on anything. Yet, as original as Price's stance is, it also appears smug and limited. For instance, one senses that while the rest of America is swallowing television whole, the Mustian family, along with a number of other country-raised southerners, are the only ones watching with any degree of intelligence and discrimination. Price sometimes seems guilty of loving his characters, or their way of life, too much. Another criticism is that made by Jay Tolson, who believes Price should do "far more" with the conflict he initiates between "the rural ethos of the characters, their countrified ways of seeing and saying things," and the urban world which now surrounds them. Tolson argues that "Price never gives any strong indication that the larger culture (television, jobs . . .) plays a part in the Beavers' crisis," which makes it seem as if Rosa and Wesley are living "in something close to a historical void."[44]

The plot of *Good Hearts* is fairly simple: a middle-aged mechanic, Wesley Beavers, takes to the road, abandoning his middle-aged wife, Rosa, in Raleigh. Traveling west, Wesley drives to Nashville, where he moves in with a younger woman named Wilson who works as a radiology technician. Back in Raleigh, Rosa is raped, an event which precipitates Wesley's return home and their renewed attempt at their marriage. One could argue that the novel would be rather conventional but for one crucial element: the sympathetic depiction of an angel/rapist who appears to play some part in a Providential design. Wave Willbanks, one of the most strangely conceived rapists in litera- ture, is the novel's central enigma, and to some degree he may have been inspired by the prescription drugs Price was directed to take during the worst part of his cancer crisis. Price in fact calls *Good Hearts* his "druggy novel" and admits he does not clearly remember writing it.[45] The creation of Wave, one of Price's most mysterious characters, is either a brilliant and original stroke on the author's part or a failure which handicaps the rest of the novel.

It would appear most reviewers of *Good Hearts* would argue for the latter. Though the novel earned a largely appreciative reception, a number of reviewers were surprised, baffled, and even angered by Price's depiction of Wave and the rape. Vince Aletti wrote, "Price's attempt to understand the inner life of Rosa's gentle rapist, and relate that boy's yearning to the univer- sal quest for love, dissolves in fatuity."[46] Gail Caldwell argued that *Good Hearts* "falters badly" when one meets the rapist and that Price's depiction of Wave as "the victim of a misguided pathology" is "unsettling stuff." Caldwell went on to argue that Price's good-heartedness, his "turn-the-other-cheek beneficence" toward Wave is puzzling.[47] Sven Birkets wrote of how the element of the rape and rapist "strains our credulity," and even more sympathetic critics such as Lee Lescaze wrote that "Mr. Price carries good-heartedness about as far as it can go."[48] For some readers then, the character of Wave, along with Price's attitude toward him, damages the credibility of the novel. Yet one should keep in mind that Price is drawn to the slightly unexplainable and is willing to take chances when it comes to the supernatural. The question is whether his risks pay off.

The first major risk which Price takes, and one hardly discussed by reviewers, involves the suggestion of a supernatural identity and mission for Wave. Price is wise enough to keep things mysterious so that the reader is never quite certain of who or what Wave is. He could simply be a deranged criminal, or an angel, or even a reincarnation of Rosa's dead father. If Wave is indeed an angel, he fits many of the traditional criteria: he is portrayed anthropomorphically, as a man in his twenties who has dropped out of N.C. State and is currently working in a textbook store; he is a stranger arriving in a time of difficulty and danger, offering what he believes to be rescue; he converses with God and serves as God's messenger; he speaks "strange sentences plainly to the ceiling" and at one point "wave[s] both long arms beside him like wings, the angel wings he saw so often in the night in dreams or awake above him in the dark overhead" (206, 274).

As an angel, Wave ostensibly plays a role in a larger design, an agent of Providence. His arrival in Rosa's bedroom is seem-

ingly triggered by Wesley's abandonment of his wife. Though
Wesley's absence has made it easier for Wave to violate Rosa,
who is now living alone, Price is suggesting something greater
and more mystical, a telepathic cause-and- effect between
Wesley's thoughts and Wave's actions. At the very moment on
New Year's Eve in 1985 in which Wesley gets into bed with
Wilson in Nashville and denies his love of Rosa, Rosa is raped in
Raleigh: "Wesley's sudden doubt set free that instant in Raleigh
the one living man who meant to harm Rosacoke's own body"
(68). Though the connection between these two events makes
sense on a metaphoric and perhaps even extrasensory level, Price
is suggesting that a creator and his design are at work. Wave is an
angel whose mission ostensibly is to reunite Rosa and Wesley,
and his actions, inappropriate and unorthodox as they seem for an
angel, nevertheless achieve an ultimate goodness: Wesley returns from Nashville and reconciles with Rosa. One wonders
whether Wesley would have returned to Rosa had Wave not
raped her.

Like Milton, who sought to "justify the ways of God to men,"
Price is perhaps attempting something similar—to account for an
evil, the act of rape. Price offers a glimpse of God's inscrutable
and mysterious will, which the author was experiencing firsthand
when he wrote this novel in the mid-1980s. Just as Price came to
see his own lengthy and horrific battle with cancer as a strange
gift which made his life better, Rosa's rape in some odd way has
saved her marriage. In effect, Price has provided one explanation
for why there is pain and suffering.

Wave, though, is not necessarily a real angel; he may instead
be a reincarnation of Rosa's dead father Horatio. At the end of
Good Hearts, Wave finds a picture of Rosa's father as a boy (the

same picture Rosa studied in *A Long and Happy Life*), and he feels a strange connection and resemblance to the boy: "Could it someway be him. . . ? Had he lived back there a whole life ago? . . . Was it why he'd felt so drawn to her life?" (273). Though such a moment has more in common with Stephen King's *The Shining,* Price maintains a level of ambiguity to hold on to his credibility. Perhaps Wave is a reincarnation of Horatio Mustian and is committing incest with his daughter; perhaps there is some mysterious and invisible connection between these two men and Rosa; or perhaps Wave is terribly misguided and has ludicrous ideas. Another possibility is that Wave is neither angel nor reincarnation, but simply a human being who serves an angelic role. Whichever the case, one should not feel frustrated by the ambiguity surrounding Wave's identity since Price's purpose is to alert the reader to supernatural possibilities.

Price's second major risk, and the one which most baffled and irritated reviewers, involves his treatment of the act of rape, which goes against everything popular psychology affirms. Whereas rape is typically viewed as an act of violence, Wave appears to be a gentle, Good Samaritan rapist who administers to needy and lonely women, providing them with attention, service, and much-needed sex. Wave even has this strange conception of himself as a man with "this gift to give, this permanent pleasure, the actual worship that all women dream of"; in other words, Wave thinks he is doing women a favor by raping them (188). At this point almost any other author would expose Wave as a misguided fool or deranged criminal, but Price does not, though he also does not eliminate that possibility: "Was his whole life wrong, founded on some sad or ridiculous mistake?" (206).

Instead Price suggests there may be some truth to Wave's strange brand of thinking, and he molds Wave into a character not wholly undeserving of one's sympathy—which is what has led to the criticism.

One way to understand Price's sympathetic attitude toward Wave is simply to acknowledge that like all human beings, if indeed he is human, Wave has a rationale for his actions which, at least in his own mind, provides justification. Price does not excuse Wave's actions but instead is simply trying to understand how the mind of this one particular rapist works.

In addition, through Wave and Wesley, Price suggests a rather startling, and certainly politically incorrect, correspondence between rape and consensual sex. Wave and Wesley are both depicted as men in need who believe they have a special gift to give women. The primary difference between them, however, is that Wesley is a more socially attuned creature who can use his looks and goodness to draw women into his bed and satisfy his urgent needs. Wave, who lacks all social grace and has misguided notions about women, must enter by force and without explicit permission. In the parallel scenes of intercourse which take place on New Year's Eve—between Wave and Rosa, Wesley and Wilson—Price reveals surprising similarities. Wave and Wesley are both described as being forceful and aggressive in their actions, and they are looking to satisfy their tremendous and overwhelming need in the bodies of strangers. In addition, both feel they are giving these women "the thing they'd missed—their body worshiped" (69). From the perspective of the women, there is fear: Rosa is "scared cold" while the rapist "roots" upon her, and Wilson has a feeling that "there was something more than a little scary in being at the mercy of someone this big and strong who seemed to need precisely *her* and *now*" (69). An intense appetite feeds both men, and though the appetite is overwhelming and frightening to the women, it is also somehow appealing. Though Rosa does not enjoy being violated by Wave, Price suggests that perhaps some of the other women whom Wave has raped did.

Price's vision here is likely to get him into trouble. Some critics may think he is saying that women like being raped, which is a reduction and distortion of his views. Instead he seems to be suggesting that the distinct line between rape and consensual sex may not be as clear and as well-defined as one imagines, that the needs of human sexuality are often more physically aggressive and devouring than one might wish to admit, and that it is a great failing in marriage not to make good use of the gift of one's own body. Though *Good Hearts* is not one of Price's best novels, it is nevertheless original and strangely audacious.

CHAPTER THREE

A Great Circle

The Mayfield Trilogy

Though Price had no idea in 1975, the year in which *The Surface of Earth* was published, that he would write two additional volumes forming a trilogy entitled *A Great Circle,* he must have realized, as he explained in an interview in 1981, that "once you start a family thing, you're into a very seductive river, because very few families have ever totally died out. The genetic material keeps going."[1] The Mayfield family, whose progress Price charts over a period of ninety years, falls into serious danger of extinction in the third volume of the trilogy; however, the genetic material, if not the surname, of this small-town white southern family continues in the most surprising of places: the character of Raven Bondurant, a black child living in the suburbs of New York City.

Though *The Surface of Earth* was given a strongly polarized reception—praised by some as a great accomplishment, a major American novel, yet panned by others as an old-fashioned, long-winded "archaic beast"—Price followed it in 1981 with *The Source of Light,* a novel less ambitious in scope but more intense in its focus. Sixteen more books and fourteen years passed, though, before Price returned to the Mayfields with *The Promise of Rest* (1995), marking the twentieth anniversary of the publication of *Surface.* Though the Mayfield novels are not Price's most popular works—they are more ponderous and demanding, at times unrelenting—they represent, up to this point in time, his greatest achievement.

As a trilogy, *A Great Circle* differs in several respects from Price's other multivolume series about a family, the Mustian novels. Despite their status as independent, self- contained narratives, the Mayfield volumes are closely interconnected in regard to theme and plot, and form an organic whole. The Mustian novels, on the other hand, are far less dependent upon one another, functioning more as separate stories which just so happen to use the same characters and setting. In addition, whereas the Mustian novels focus on a single generation of characters (Rosacoke, Wesley, and Milo), the Mayfield novels are concerned with the passage of time and with the way six generations of a family evolve over ninety years, a period covering almost the entire twentieth century. In *A Great Circle* Price's scope expands dramatically as he reveals, in a grand manner resembling Tolstoy or even the Bible, just how much the forces of history, family, and geneticism shape the lives of individuals. Finally, whereas the Mustians are primarily upper lower-class and rural, the Mayfields and Kendals of *A Great Circle,* who have more in common with Price's own extended family, are middle-class and relatively well-educated. Though even Price's most uneducated characters possess a natural wisdom, his central character in *A Great Circle,* Hutch Mayfield, reveals an attempt to tell a story about an individual as educated and as psychologically complex as the writer himself.

The grand theme of *A Great Circle* is love, though certainly not a joyful, sentimental, or romantic love. Instead, Price's brand turns out to be rather dark, obsessive, and consuming in nature.

A GREAT CIRCLE

From the dual events which open *The Surface of Earth*—the recounted suicide of Thad Watson upon the death of his wife, Katherine, and the elopement of Eva Kendal and Forrest Mayfield—to the passionate homosexual union of Wade Mayfield and Wyatt Bondurant which dominates *The Promise of Rest,* love stands as the central and dominant force in the trilogy. Yet as one sees in each of these instances, love can be far more destructive than nurturing: Thad's love literally kills his wife (she dies in childbirth), which then triggers his suicide; Forrest's love for Eva begins a wave of destruction which will continue for generations; and the love between Wade and Wyatt, though more joyful and mutual than perhaps any other in the trilogy, literally consumes their bodies by transmitting the virus that causes AIDS.

In addition to its devouring nature, Price's brand of love demands great risk and sacrifice. Both Eva in 1903 and Wade in the 1980s sacrifice their relationships with their fathers, the most important person in their lives up to that point, in order to be with their lovers; yet whereas Eva leaves her husband and returns to her father after just a year, Wade stays with his lover, Wyatt, both in life and death. In this regard, Wade may suggest an end to the Mayfield demon or curse which has made it so difficult for these men to create fulfilling relationships outside of their own families.

What is perhaps most striking about Price's depiction of love in *A Great Circle,* beyond its devastation, is that it comes in so many forms: between man and woman, man and man, woman and woman, black and white, parent and child. Though popular culture tends to be fixated on romantic heterosexual love, Price's Mayfield novels demonstrate that love is a good deal more complex and diverse than one might imagine. For instance, the line between hetero- and homosexuality, which seems so absolute in contemporary American culture, blurs in Price's work, leading the reader to question the divisions that have been created. Though Hutch Mayfield has been married for nearly forty years to a woman, the most intensely satisfying erotic experience in his life was with a man, Strawson Stuart, when both were young.

Since *A Long and Happy Life* Price's readers have been aware of his ability to depict heterosexual love. The real achievement of *A Great Circle,* in contrast, is Price's ability to limn other intense forms of love. Few writers deal as well and as fully with parent-child love as Price, particularly as those bonds impede, complicate, and sometimes prevent a character's formation of other adult relationships. Price demonstrates that a degree of eroticism exists between parent and child, yet he does not, like others, sensationalize those emotions by offering lurid scenes of incest and abuse; instead he demonstrates that such eroticism is natural though potentially dangerous if unrestrained.

For many of Price's characters—Eva Kendal, Forrest Mayfield, Hutch Mayfield—their relationship with their fathers is the most significant bond in their lives. Eva's devotion to her father tears her from her new husband and returns her to her family for the next sixty years. Forrest finds himself largely handicapped for the first thirty years of his life because of his supposed failure to satisfy his father when he was a child. And Hutch's early interest in young men has much to do with his desire to recover and vicariously love an image of his young father. Certainly the most central and urgent relationship in each of the three novels is between fathers and sons, with father-son reunions figuring as the recurring event to which the narratives lead. In *The Surface of Earth* three generations of Mayfield men—Robinson and Forrest, Forrest and Rob, and Rob and Hutch—reunite after years of separation or abandonment. In *The Source of Light* the narrative builds to Hutch's emergency return from Europe for Rob's death. And in *The Promise of Rest* Hutch and Wade are reunited so that Hutch can take care of his dying son; in addition, *Promise* literally ends with Hutch's walking hand in hand with his grandson—whom he has, in essence, just met. Each novel builds to and centers upon periods of time in which fathers and sons are given the opportunity, most often before a death, to seek mutual forgiveness and to redeem the past.

In regard to the central themes of family and love in *A Great Circle,* what stands out is how terribly unsuccessful the marriages are. Eva and Forrest remain together barely a year and send pain down through generations; Bedford and Charlotte Kendal do not touch one another for fifteen years; and Hutch and Ann Mayfield spend nearly forty years together in a union which becomes a living death. In contrast, the more unconventional families are far better at creating loving relationships. For instance, Forrest Mayfield, while still technically married to Eva, spends the last thirty-five years of his life in mutual contentment with his father's former lover and housekeeper, Polly Drewry. In addition, the homosexual union between Wade Mayfield and Wyatt Bondurant proves to be one of the most satisfying and passionate in the trilogy, with Wade and Wyatt even playing a role in the creation of a child through Wyatt's sister Ivory, who functions to some degree as a part of their intimate family. Though Price has not set out to trash or destroy the traditional family, the Mayfield

novels reveal the failings of such a family while offering powerful and original alternatives. To this extent, *A Great Circle*
legitimizes, even endorses, unconventional families and living
arrangements.

In light of these problematic marriages and families, many
of the children in the trilogy—Charlotte Watson, Forrest Mayfield,
Rob Mayfield, Hutch Mayfield, Raven Bondurant—find themselves raised not by their natural parents but by a surrogate or by
a community of willing and loving adults, which sometimes
includes one of their natural parents. For instance, Rob Mayfield
is raised by his Aunt Rena; his mother, Eva; and the Kendal
family cook, Sylvie. Raven Bondurant is raised primarily by his
grandmother Lucy Patterson Bondurant and his mother, Ivory.
Though most of the children in *A Great Circle* are raised in a
loving fashion—no real Dickensian orphans here—they tend to
be obsessed with one of their natural parents, most often the
missing one. Bankey Patterson, Forrest Mayfield, Rob Mayfield,
and Hutch Mayfield all devote a great deal of energy in searching—either physically, or spiritually through dreams—for a
missing mother or father. Such a quest is archetypal, and for many
of these characters, peace of mind is not possible until they locate
that lost person or come to terms with the absence.

What one begins to notice about Price's trilogy, particularly
in regard to the relationship between parents and children, is its
circularity. History repeats itself; successive generations of
Mayfields and Kendals find themselves facing the same decisions and problems which plagued their parents and grandparents. Price reveals the circular nature of family life through
patterns and repetitions stretching over six generations. In this

respect *A Great Circle* is an appropriate title for the trilogy; not only does it reflect the circularity of the Mayfield family history, but in its navigational sense it sheds light on the tragic course of the Mayfield men. The term *a great circle,* Price writes, "refers to the shortest distance between any two points on the surface of a globe—a route that, with all their waste and recklessness, the Mayfields in their passion generally take."[2] In addition, the term relates to the "surface/center" metaphor which plays such a significant role in the trilogy. Price's characters are continually searching and yearning for a center which offers peace and rest, and presumably that center is at the core of the earth.

If love, sexuality, and family are at the center of *A Great Circle,* then these themes are enriched and intensified by Price's consideration of race. Throughout the Mayfield novels, whites and blacks are seen living and working in close daily proximity, and the forces of attraction and discord between the two races are powerful. Much of that attraction is erotic, leading to sexual relationships between blacks and several generations of white Mayfield men: Robinson Mayfield has a history of what he calls "niggering around"; Rob Mayfield is sexually involved with the Hutchins' black servant Della; and Wade Mayfield is sexually involved with Ivory Bondurant before he meets and then falls in love with her brother, Wyatt. In addition, these relationships often produce racially mixed offspring. Grainger Walters, the central black figure in the trilogy and the grandson of Robinson Mayfield, is at least one-quarter white, and Raven Bondurant, the son of Wade Mayfield, is more than one-half white.

Yet eroticism is not the only attachment linking blacks to whites in *A Great Circle.* There is also, as Price demonstrates, a tremendous degree of care, goodness, friendship, and mutuality existing between the races—even in the American South during the middle part of the twentieth century.[3] Certainly the friendship between Rob Mayfield and Grainger Walters is unlike almost any in American literature; these two men, one black and one white (though related by blood), feel tremendous devotion and love toward one another, and their bonds push beyond the limitations set down by racial custom.

The attachment between blacks and whites is not, however, an equal one. In *A Great Circle,* which reflects twentieth-century American culture, blacks exist largely to serve whites. Not only do blacks work as domestic employees (cook, driver, household servant), but they also serve, and this is unique to Price's work, as "angels." Blacks are angels in the Greek sense of being messengers: they deliver vital messages to the white characters at significant moments in their lives. To a large extent the black characters in *A Great Circle* are morally superior to their white employers and possess forms of wisdom the whites lack, yet the blacks have their own problems, which often reflect upon those facing the white characters. Ultimately the blacks are sacrificial and redemptive characters in that a sizable part of their existence is devoted to making life easier for the whites. Each day blacks tend to the domestic chores and the child-rearing of white families, spreading their wisdom and delivering messages, and then each night they are exiled to their smaller rooms and poorer circumstances.

Price suggests, though, that there will be a price to pay for this history of inequality. Black militants like Wyatt Bondurant epitomize the resentment and hostility of the black community, and such an attitude might eventually find expression in Grainger Walters's words to Hutch Mayfield, "Colored men bearing down on you tonight, big knives in their fist."[4] The burning and fire imagery in *The Promise of Rest,* which relates mostly to AIDS, also bears racial significance; blacks have been sacrificially burned throughout history, and the result may one day be a revolutionary, racial bonfire which will transform America. The hope against such a conflagration lies in the continued mixing of racial blood, which may help to bridge the gap between blacks and whites, and Raven Bondurant is the embodiment of that hope. Though the trilogy ends with another Mayfield man's being raised largely by black women, this particular Mayfield man carries the skin color and surname of an African-American female. The long attraction between the Mayfields and the blacks resolves in the expiration of the white Mayfield line and the continuation of the black Bondurant line; the genetic material of the Mayfields has been absorbed into black culture.

The Surface of Earth

Twenty years after its publication, *The Surface of Earth* remains Price's most ambitious effort. Though it has sold fewer copies and received less enthusiastic reviews than either *A Long and Happy Life* or *Kate Vaiden,* it is still Price's "big book," announcing itself as a work aspiring to greatness through its grand vision, complexity, and literal size—nearly twice the length of a typical Price novel. Michael Brondoli writes, "*The Surface of Earth* . . . reveals every authentic mark of a work that will stand for a good long while, one of our deepest plotted soundings of human grief." And Michael Kreyling concurs by stating, "It would not be a gross overstatement to claim that . . . *The Surface of Earth* . . . is one of the more significant American novels of the twentieth century."[5] Though the American literary community has not granted such a distinction to *Surface,* it will likely receive more attention since it now stands as the first volume of a trilogy, a family saga stretching for more than eleven hundred pages.

In seeking most fully to understand *The Surface of Earth,* one should study its critical reception in 1975. Appearing at a time in which more experimental novels were in vogue—winners of the National Book Award in fiction for 1973, 1974, and 1976 were respectively Barth's *Chimera,* Pynchon's *Gravity's Rainbow,* and Gaddis's *JR*—*Surface* was deemed to be out of step with contemporary literary fashion.[6] In a now-notorious review which appeared on the front page of the *New York Times Book Review* (and which apparently played some role, both positive and negative, in many subsequent reviews), Richard Gilman attacked Price's novel for being "old-fashioned," referring to it as "a great lumbering archaic beast," "a mastodon sprung to life from beneath an ice-field." Gilman's point was that a semi-realistic novel dealing with family life and obsessive love in the South had already been done so often that it had become extinct. According to Gilman, Price was not allowing contemporary literary fashion to play a role in his novel, and he faulted Price for not attempting to include those elements which had indeed become fashionable, such as "the wit and humor we have been accustomed to in recent fiction . . . the pure verbal play or desperate jest stemming from a sense of the embattled relations between writing itself and life."[7]

A GREAT CIRCLE

Gilman's arguments seem as absurd today as they did to a number of writers and critics in 1975. Eudora Welty wrote an angry letter to the editor of the *Times* which appeared, along with Gilman's response, several weeks later; and Shaun O'Connell denounced Gilman in the *Massachusetts Review.*[8] However, Gilman's stance reveals the kind of critical climate into which some of Price's writings have been delivered. No matter the quality of Price's work, certain influential critics will argue that another novel by a southerner about family and love is obsolete, and that narrative which is not postmodern, ironic, and playful is hardly worth one's time.

Beyond the review by Gilman, there were other criticisms of *Surface* which bear consideration: it is too long; the language is formal and artificial; Price's grand scheme is contrived and organized to the extent it does not allow for surprise; Price's characters sound too much alike, lacking variety of pitch; so much of the action takes place offstage; the novel has a static quality because Price overanalyzes and holds moments up to microscopic observation. All of these points bear some truth and make the novel, for many readers, unrelenting and irritating, yet the same criticisms apply to many of the great works of literature. For instance, the language of *Paradise Lost* is formal and its scheme grand; much of Dickens, Tolstoy, and Richardson is too long; and most of the action in Greek drama takes place offstage. It is important to bear in mind two points: first, that the contemporary environment favors a more idiomatic, casual, and realistic brand of literature than Price writes; and second, that Price, who studied Milton and Greek drama at Oxford, and who was actually translating stories from the Bible in preparation for *Surface,* is a writer working in the classical tradition. Gilman was absolutely correct in viewing Price as a writer operating outside the bounds of literary fashion, yet he was wrong to assume that that was any kind of weakness or shortcoming on Price's part.

The best way to approach *The Surface of Earth* is through the same mind set one would use to approach the Bible, Milton, or Greek drama. This is not to say that Price's novel equals the achievement of these canonical works, but merely to suggest it has more in common with such works than it does with the writings of Pynchon, Gaddis, or Barth. When reading the Bible or Milton, one accepts that the speech of the characters is often more formal or literary than real, yet that does not damage the work. The same principle should apply to a good, classically trained, contemporary writer like Price, whose characters may speak in an unrealistic manner. As Fred Chappell explains, "[Price's] characters share a mode of speech which is contiguous to 'normal' speech, but which differs from it sharply in including as important basics the use of ellipsis (because of shared emotional knowledge) and the use of a certain formalism."[9] Chappell refers to ellipsis as a "single hallmark of Price's style," and he demonstrates how it functions in a conversation between Rob Mayfield and his adolescent son, Hutch, who is trying to understand their past:

> Hutch said, "What was the promise?—just to change your life?" . . .
> "To stop harming people in the ways I had, by not touching one human body again (not for my old reasons), by not drinking liquor; I had drunk a lot of that since I was your age."

"Why?"

"A form of ether, deadens the pain."

Hutch said, "But you promised that *if* we two lived, Rachel *and* I. You got just half."

"That was why I asked you; you were all that was left. I thought you should say. I thought you might be taken if I broke it."

"And I told you Yes?"

"In your sleep, age three."

"Did you listen?" Hutch said.

"Obey, you mean?" Rob stopped in his tracks.[10]

As Chappell points out, once the reader arrives at Hutch's line "You got just half," the ellipsis starts: "They begin to speak inchoate love lyrics, to talk in highly charged tropes, and to reveal secrets not even the reader has known till now."[11] The reader must work to interpret the private communication between father and son as it takes place in a language of code words and unstated acknowledgments. Price's dialogue, of course, is not entirely believable, yet it is no less believable than speech in, say, Shakespeare, Milton, or Eugene O'Neill. Thus, when critics deride Price for creating speech which is formal and artificial, what they may actually mean is that it is not fashionable, casual, or colloquial.

With further regard to the nature of speech in *Surface,* we may say that Price is attempting what many of the great writers before him have: to create a new language. Any page from *Surface* reveals Price's own signature style, in which characters speak in a heightened, intense form of English. Price creates this effect not only through ellipsis but through spareness and the heavy use of Anglo-Saxon words. Defining his style as "the paradoxically baroque plain-style," Price said in a 1978 interview, "I think I write the most Anglo-Saxon English currently being written in America, but it's also very baroque."[12] Though the baroque accounts for his often lengthy and elaborate sentences, Constance Rooke writes that Price's prose has "a muscular, abrupt quality which we associate with Anglo-Saxon," and she demonstrates his "heavy reliance upon a core vocabulary" of words which are Anglo-Saxon rather than Latin in origin: *"protect, shield, threat, lethal, pain, loss, perfect, permanent, misery, pardon, plea, promise, blame, waste, warn, amends, ruin, error, wish, desperate, receipt, goal, gift, want, need, food, suck,* and *famine."*[13] Though many of these words are visible in earlier Price fiction, one witnesses in *Surface* the maturity of his unique prose; the colloquial richness of *A Long and Happy Life* and *A Generous Man* gracefully blends with the spareness of *Love and Work* and *Permanent Errors.*

In addition to their remarks concerning Price's use of speech and language, critics have rightfully complained about the grand scheme in *Surface,* suggesting it is contrived, artificial, and repetitious. For instance, three successive generations of Mayfield men desert their sons; childbirth accounts for the death or near-death of seemingly every pregnant female in the novel; characters unknowingly share the same specific dreams and nightmares with other characters; blacks continually appear as "angels" to whites, delivering messages and bringing redemption; and numerous characters have at the center of their emotional lives their relationships with their fathers. Though much of this seems

A GREAT CIRCLE

forced and unrealistic, Price has a greater objective: to demonstrate how dreams, emotions, needs, desires, and even actions are transmitted genetically between family members over generations. Family situations reenact themselves, and descendants are often faced with the same decisions and choices as their parents and grandparents. Though Price may appear heavy-handed in his parallels and repetitions, one must not necessarily demand absolute realism on the writer's part. As Christopher Lehmann-Haupt explains, "through the story's insistent repetition, a composite emerges—a fusion of all the women who have suffered in childbirth and all the men who turn to Negro 'angels' to assuage their guilt." Lehmann-Haupt then goes on to call the composite "monumental and tragically heroic."[14] Price's novel is not about a particular individual; it is a collective story which works through repetition, a circular story which builds upon stories which came before.

The Surface of Earth is primarily about families and the way the actions, flawed choices, consuming passions, and emotional problems of one family member affect future generations. Price demonstrates that actions have consequences which go far beyond the individual, turning up in the lives of children, grandchildren, and future descendants. In Price's work, family often operates like fate, exerting a nearly inescapable pressure upon the choices of individuals.

The novel, which focuses upon the Mayfield and Kendal families between 1903 and 1944, begins with a scene immersed in family life. The Kendal children are sitting on their front porch, the very locus of stories and family exchange, when they ask their father for *the* story about their grandparents, Thad Watson and

Katherine Epps Watson. The secret story, of which they have only heard "scraps," accounts for the birth of their mother, Charlotte Watson Kendal, and the death of their grandparents. The story is significant because as Eva, the oldest daughter, says, "It's our own story." It is a story which contributes to the identity of the family, revealing to the children the nature of their heritage: the intensity, violence, and harm which their ancestors wreaked upon one another. Though Price has said, "it seems melodramatic to call it a curse" and opts for the term *demon,* one certainly suspects that the story will exert some lasting influence upon this family. As Price has asserted, "[*Surface*] is about how one generation can start something that causes pain, suffering, even tragedy over three or four generations, coming finally to rest, to a solution through time and change."[15]

Fittingly, the story of the Kendal children's grandparents, the primal story, is told not on any casual evening but on the very night when Eva Kendal will leave home to elope with her Latin teacher, Forrest Mayfield, who is twice her age. Though Eva has already decided to elope before hearing this story, Price draws the reader toward connections between the generations. The careful reader will notice that Eva's father, Bedford Kendal, has already said to his children, "I hope none of you lives to face such a choice [as your grandfather had]," the choice ostensibly between child or mate—living on with one's child, or dying in order to be with one's dead spouse. Provoked by his children's lack of respect—they refer to their grandfather and mother as killers—Bedford then adds prophetically, "But one of you will." Beyond the mysteriousness of Bedford's response, Price forces the reader to ponder the consequences of this primal act for future generations.

A GREAT CIRCLE

Will Eva and her siblings, along with their descendants, face similar situations and make similar choices? As it turns out, Eva's son, Rob, will face the same predicament as Thad Watson, yet he will opt to live on with his new child. And Eva too will find herself in many ways repeating the lives of her female ancestors: like her grandmother Katherine, she will offer herself to an eager and impatient man, with their act of love nearly killing her in childbirth; and like her mother, Charlotte, she will unintentionally cause her own mother's death. One also wonders how Eva's decision—to abandon her family and later her husband—will affect future generations of Mayfields. The opening of *Surface* resembles Genesis in that one is prepared for the unfolding events of the narrative by first having witnessed a couple's fall from grace. Though Forrest and Eva appear to be the novel's Adam and Eve, one could argue that the truly original fallen couple is Thad and Katherine.

Since *The Surface of Earth* does not have a central character or even couple, one must consider other ways of defining the critical focus of the narrative. One option is to view the novel as the story of the problematic blending of two families, Mayfield and Kendal. Another is to read the novel as the story of Mayfield fathers and sons: Robinson, Forrest, Rob, Hutch, and to some extent Grainger, who is Robinson's black grandson. Though Eva remains a significant character throughout the novel, and though other women such as Polly Drewry, Rena Kendal, and Della play sizable roles, it is the men who dominate. Each of the novel's three sections revolves around the life of a single Mayfield man and builds to the moment when he is reunited with his father. Book One ultimately becomes Forrest's story, culminating in his reunion with his father Robinson and his ensuing decision to proceed with his life. Book Two is Rob Mayfield's story, detailing his coming-of-age, his courtship and marriage, his reunion with his father, and the conception of his son. And Book Three is Hutch Mayfield's story, in which he and his father Rob spend a few days together traveling in June of 1944.

Book One, entitled "Absolute Pleasures," reveals the damage that can be inflicted upon family members and descendants when an individual seeks some "absolute pleasure," usually sexual in nature. In this opening book Thad Watson, Forrest Mayfield, Eva Kendal, and Robinson Mayfield all harm others in attempting to satisfy themselves: Thad "kills" his wife by pressuring her into having a child; Forrest destroys the stability of the Kendal family by stealing Eva; Eva "kills" her mother and devastates her family by eloping; and Robinson damages his son and others through abandonment.

The two major actions of Book One are Forrest and Eva's elopement and short-lived union, and the ensuing journey which leads Forrest to his father. Though Forrest is "drowning in gratitude" for his young wife, Eva quickly becomes disillusioned with her husband and plagued with guilt for having abandoned her family. After nearly dying in childbirth—she fears her grandmother's story is repeating itself—Eva receives a devastating blow: her mother, repeating the act of her own father, commits suicide. With her newborn son, Rob, Eva then leaves Forrest's home in Bracey, Virginia, and returns to the Kendal family home in Fontaine, North Carolina, where she will care for her father and atone for her mistake.

Rejected and alone, Forrest returns to Panacea Springs and finds the springs, like his marriage, in disrepair. While there, he

A GREAT CIRCLE

meets a vagabond, an elderly black man named Bankey Patterson, born a slave in the 1820s. Through the example of Bankey, who is searching for his mother, Forrest is inspired to search for his father, who abandoned Forrest when he was five. Though Bankey's role may seem insignificant, it becomes intriguing over the course of the trilogy to see how the relationship between the Patterson and Mayfield families persists. Twenty years later Della, a Hutchins' family servant and a descendant of Bankey, will help ease Rob Mayfield's pain and yearning by welcoming him into her bed; more than fifty years later in *The Source of Light* another female descendant of Bankey will assist Ann Gatlin, Hutch's girlfriend at the time, with an abortion; and more than eighty years later in *The Promise of Rest* Wade Mayfield, Hutch's son, will become sexually involved with two of Bankey's descendants, Ivory and Wyatt Bondurant. In fact, the final descendant in the Mayfield line and the hope for the future, Raven Bondurant, is actually a mixture of Patterson, Mayfield, and Bondurant blood. The black Pattersons and white Mayfields have a long, though nearly invisible, history with one another in which the Pattersons have played an assisting and comforting role for the Mayfields, and fittingly the trilogy ends with the two families' sharing in the creation of a child.

Searching for his father, Forrest eventually locates Robinson in the Mayfield family home in Richmond, where he is living with Polly Drewry, a much younger woman who is common-law wife to the older man. Though his reunion with his father is hardly joyful or satisfying, Forrest appears to have freed himself from the intense guilt and need which have handicapped him for so long. In addition, the book ends with two significant events: Forrest's gift of the Mayfield family ring to Grainger Walters, which begins a quasi marriage between Grainger and several generations of Mayfield men; and the death of Robinson (throughout the trilogy, a father's death functions as one of the most liberating events in his son's life).

Book Two, entitled "The Heart in Dreams," leaps sixteen years forward to the time when Rob Mayfield is on the verge of manhood and flight. This book is the story of Rob, who not only shares his grandfather's first name—the death of Robinson Sr. is followed almost immediately by the emergence of a new adolescent Rob—but repeats many of the patterns established by his ancestors. Like his grandmother Charlotte, Rob knows his birth caused harm, nearly killing his mother; and like his father, Forrest, he believes he has been deprived and neglected by his parents. Rob also resembles his mother through both his strong attachment to a single parent—namely, to his mother—and his simultaneous desire to escape that parent and his entire family.

Much of this book deals with Rob's journey away from Fontaine, a journey which mirrors that of his father, Forrest. Like Forrest, Rob ultimately discovers some answers, acquires a mate, and reunites with his father in Richmond. Yet Rob also resembles his grandfather Robinson through his strong passion for drink and flesh, which leads Forrest to advise his son, "Change now while you can. Find someone to help you and start your life" (201). Rob takes his father's advice by returning to Goshen and choosing Rachel Hutchins as a wife. Rachel, who had years before induced a psychosomatic pregnancy, soon becomes pregnant with Hutch, but as Price reveals in advance, the birth of this child will kill its mother.

Book Three, entitled "Partial Amends"—Rob's attempt at making amends to those souls he and his forebears have harmed—

contains the story that Price had truly been wanting to tell since 1961. Originally Price had imagined writing a novel about an alcoholic salesman father and his son, traveling during the summer months of World War II; however, he was "balked" in that effort for more than a decade. Not until he saw that "this new and growing story required, simply and frighteningly, that I return to its source" was Price able to write the novel.[16] Thus, in order to tell the father-and-son story that dominates Book Three, Price had to go back more than forty years into the past and generate what became the first three hundred pages of *The Surface of Earth.*

The focus now turns to Hutch Mayfield, who at fourteen follows the pattern established by his father and grandmother: departure from the Kendal family home in Fontaine in hopes of finding something better. Though Hutch is more composed and disciplined than his male Mayfield ancestors, he shares their need for solitude and their questing spirit, both of which propel him toward fulfilling his ambition of becoming an artist—one who will be able to know and use the past in order to redeem it. Because he was abandoned by his father and fears his father blames him for having "killed" his mother, Hutch greatly desires a future for Rob and himself: "I've waited for you since I was five years old—to come back and take me to live with you, to find us a place" (390). Hutch's love for his father is intense, yet it is complicated by both his father's drinking and Min Tharrington's design to marry Rob.

The journey which Hutch and Rob take through Virginia, as the liberating events of D day occur across the ocean, is what Hutch hopes will be the beginning of their new life together. However, when they are visiting Polly Drewry in Richmond, Rob falls into a drunken state and collapses naked on the floor—an incident which drives Hutch away from Richmond toward his maternal grandfather, Raven Hutchins, in Goshen. Once there, Hutch learns of his grandfather's recent death, but conversely he encounters people who once knew his mother and have stories to tell of her. In particular he meets Alice Matthews, the former companion to his mother, who serves as a mentor to Hutch in his quest to become an artist. Together they sketch landscapes, and Alice gives Hutch a lesson in the art of seeing—a lesson that sheds light on the novel's title. Alice informs Hutch of how "the secrets of God" exist beneath the surface of earth, the landscape he is currently sketching. Hutch realizes that through patience, watchfulness, and assuming the state of mind of an artist, he can penetrate beneath that surface toward a core. Of the novel's title, Price has explained that his characters "are perversely and tragically and comically insisting upon living on the surface of earth as opposed to anywhere near the center of what the earth might contain, the center of the possibilities of love both human and divine which the earth would seem to offer them."[17] Price's characters suffer because they are not in touch with that "invisible center of their lives"; they have lived primarily on the surface, seeking satisfaction solely in the bodies of others. As an aspiring artist, Hutch offers hope and redemption; perhaps he will emerge as the first Mayfield man to resist the waste of his ancestors.

The novel ends not only with the reunion of Hutch and Rob but with the passing of the Mayfield wedding ring from Grainger to Hutch. Given originally to Anna Godwin by her husband, Robinson Mayfield, the ring ties various generations of the family together and adds to the circular nature of the narrative.

A GREAT CIRCLE

Though almost buried with Anna, the ring survives because Anna's daughter, Hatt Shorter, has removed it from her hand and later passes it to her brother, Forrest. Forrest then offers it unsuccessfully to a line of unwilling recipients—Eva, Robinson, and Polly—before Grainger finally accepts it. The passing of the ring to Grainger begins a long friendship, fraternal and erotic in nature, between Grainger and the Mayfield men. Though Grainger gives the ring to his wife, Gracie, she later returns it, and thus the novel comes full circle to where Grainger passes the ring, with its mixed history—it stands as an expression of love, yet has followed a path of ruin and waste—to another Mayfield man, Hutch.

Though *The Surface of Earth* generates far more mysteries, particularly regarding characters' dreams,[18] than this study can adequately deal with, there is one unusually powerful and strange image which needs to be addressed: Forrest's "main memory" of his father, who abandoned the family when Forrest was five:

I remember. . . . that one Sunday . . . I was laid out on my little narrow bed. . . . He came in silent in a cotton nightshirt with plumcolored stripes and lay down on me; I was stretched on my back. Laid his whole weight on me. . . . and when I looked up . . . there were my father's eyes staring down at me. . . . the neediest eyes I've seen, asking me. (24)

For Forrest, and for the reader, the scene remains a mystery. What precisely did Robinson want from his young son: sexual contact?

human warmth? love? Whichever it was, Forrest is burdened with guilt because of his failure to provide for his father: "That has been the hard thing in my life—thinking of that: that after coming to me and begging for God knows what as food and getting no gift, then he wanted to go. Go away from us" (25). This initial failure to satisfy and hold on to his father leads to other failures, most notably his failure with Eva.

Variations on this scene are played out on several occasions in the novel. For instance, two generations later Rob Mayfield repeats this act with Hutch: "So Rob slowly took off his jacket and tie, unbuttoned his collar, stepped out of his shoes, and took the last steps till his legs touched the bed. Then he laid himself—full-length, dead-weight—on Hutch's body" (347). In fact, Hutch's "strongest, strangest memory," which engendered both "fear and happiness," is of his father's enacting this same ritual when Hutch was just four or five; though Hutch experienced "pleasure" during this act, there was also a fear of suffocation, a "joy that also threatened to kill him" (347). Another variation upon this act occurs in the dreams of Eva Kendal, who imagines her father as an incubus bent upon destroying the entire family during a single night:

> [her father] rolled his huge body leftward till he lay full-length on her sleeping mother—who remained asleep as he fastened his open mouth over hers and drew up each shallow breath she exhaled till she lay empty, dead. . . . performed the same smothering theft on Kennerly. . . . Then up the stairs to Rena. . . . (10)

Eva, who at this moment has escaped her father by eloping, then imagines him coming to devour her, thus ending the dream.

Despite variations, one can distinguish a common pattern in Price's depiction of the scene of the incubus: a father enters the bed of his son or daughter, lies on top of him or her, and either takes or awaits some form of nourishment. Sometimes this scene occurs in a dream, in other instances it is recalled as a childhood memory, and in still others it occurs in the present action of the novel. Mostly the scene is one which transpires between Mayfield men and their sons, and the reader most often experiences it through the sensibility of the son or passive recipient. The scene also resonates with ambiguity and mystery since the son is usually unaware of what precisely is happening and being asked of him.

Though the incubus traditionally suggests an evil spirit or demon in male form who seeks to have sexual intercourse with sleeping women, the term in modern psychological usage is less demonic and more inclusive, suggesting a nightmare of a sexual nature which gives one the feeling of being burdened with a heavy weight on the chest (the Latin *incubare* means "to lie upon"). For Ernest Jones, a student of Freud and also his biographer, the incubus, which is virtually a synonym for the term *nightmare,* is "an expression of intense mental conflict centreing about some form of 'repressed' sexual desire . . . an expression of a mental conflict over an incestuous desire."[19] Jones's observation that "the normal incest wishes of infancy" are at the center of the incubus sheds light on Price's fiction, particularly since Price follows Freud in suggesting there is "an innate bi- or polysexuality in all creatures" which for social reasons is re-pressed.[20]

To return then to Forrest's memory of his father's lying upon him, one questions what Robinson wants from his young son and in what manner he touches the boy. It may be useful to consider how a similar scene was staged in a production of Price's television drama, *Private Contentment*. Lee Yopp, the adaptor (for the stage) and director of Price's play, explained that Price had told him during a conversation that he wanted a sense of sexual ambiguity in the play's final scene between brother and sister:

> We were talking about the climax. Mr. Price said that what took place between the boy and the girl was more than just a kiss. He wasn't trying to be "cutesy" or anything. Mr. Price said that his own guess was that they don't have complete intercourse; on the other hand, they don't just embrace and walk back to the house. There must be, he said, a sense of crucial ambiguity.[21]

Perhaps "crucial ambiguity" best describes the nature of the physical intimacy between fathers and sons in Price's fiction. Though one never senses that anything approaching intercourse occurs, one cannot be absolutely sure of the nature of the contact. Robinson Mayfield does not appear to be attempting coitus with his son, nor does he give any indication of being a pedophile, yet it is suggested he wants more than merely simple and socially acceptable affection. What is unfortunate about this particular scene is that Forrest is emotionally harmed because he does not understand what his father wants.

A GREAT CIRCLE

What is perhaps most interesting about the incubus is how it passes between individuals: father to son, husband to wife. Eva—who, like Forrest, finds that her closest bond is not with a spouse or lover but with her father—is also visited by a dream in which her father appears as an incubus. The dream expresses her guilt no doubt over having abandoned her family, particularly her father, and it also answers to her fear that her father would smother and devour her if she stayed. Yet Eva, who returns to her family within a year, has a tremendous desire to be with her father, and one could interpret her dream as an expression of her desire to be "smothered" or loved by him. Eva's incubus dream occurs on her wedding night, and immediately after the dream, in which she imagines her father "fasten[ing] his open mouth" over the mouths of everyone in her immediate family, Eva turns to Forrest and assumes herself the role of the succubus: "Her hand strained out and took his shoulder and with more strength, even than before, drew him down and over her body . . . and quickly in. Then with her hands on the back of his head, she fastened his mouth over hers and endured in silence the gift she required" (11). Eva utilizes Forrest as a surrogate father and experiences the sexual relationship with her husband which she cannot have with her father. In psychological terms, Forrest offers a vehicle through which Eva can bond physically with her greatest love, her father, and at the same time punish her father by abandoning him and eloping with Forrest. Again Price demonstrates how an intense relationship between a parent and child makes it difficult if not impossible for that child to bond with others.

The deepest and healthiest attachment between parent and

child is between Rob and Hutch, and Rob describes their relationship with great emotion: "You slept in my bed from the time you could walk; and I'd lie down beside you in some dim light and watch you for minutes. . . . I loved you till it drew great tears down my cheeks" (394). Though separated for more than eight years, the reunited Rob and Hutch appear like lovers, sharing a bed, talking, sleeping, and touching. There is a distinct physical component to their companionship that begins at Hutch's conception; as Rob later explains to his son, "Rachel [Hutch's mother] pulled you out of me by main force."[22] As they lie together in bed, Hutch ponders his conception in the body of his father: "He tried to imagine his own life starting in that groin there, yearning out into Rachel fifteen years ago" (485). Though the emergence of life is typically associated with a woman's body, Price alters the perspective, reminding readers of the father's role. Hutch has literally been created from the genitals of Rob, and the two share an intimacy and trust which surpasses that of even the most constant lovers and which leads Hutch's girlfriend to say in *The Source of Light,* "You love your father more than anything else."[23]

The Source of Light

The Source of Light continues the family saga begun in *The Surface of Earth,* picking up the story of Hutch and Rob Mayfield in 1955, eleven years after the conclusion of the earlier novel. In addition to once again focusing on father-son relations, Price returns to many of the same themes—the search for erotic and familial love, the need for freedom and solitude, the yearning for rest, the circular pattern of life—and same narrative techniques: the use of letters, dreams, short intense scenes. Yet *The Source of Light* is a different kind of novel. Whereas *The Surface of Earth* covers more than forty years of time and has a grand and evolving cast of major characters, *The Source of Light* is narrower in its sweep, tracing just ten months in the life of Hutch Mayfield, now a twenty-five-year-old aspiring poet bound for study in Europe. *The Source of Light* is less concerned with the passage of time (years, generations) and more interested in how a young man survives a critical passage in his life, one in which he takes his first step toward becoming an artist while simultaneously experiencing the crushing yet liberating death of his father. Whereas *The Surface of Earth* is a family saga, *The Source of Light* comes closest to being a *künstlerroman,* or a portrait of the artist.

In addition to this central contrast in scope, other differences in regard to setting and sexuality exist between the two novels. For instance, whereas *Surface* is set almost exclusively in rural North Carolina and Virginia, much of *The Source of Light* takes place in Europe: the urban centers of Oxford and Rome, the countryside of Wales and the Scilly Islands. Of Price's ten novels, this is the only one set largely in a specific locale which is not the South;[24] one might even call *The Source of Light* Price's Oxford novel since it reflects upon his stay there as a Rhodes scholar and is dedicated to his English teachers and friends, David Cecil and Stephen Spender. As for the other noticeable difference, namely the novel's treatment of sexuality, Price offers his most candid portrayal of homosexuality yet. Though there are hints of homosexual interest in *Surface*—Thorne Bradley's affection for Rob, Alice Matthews's love for Rachel—

Price openly reveals in *The Source of Light* that Hutch has male lovers from whom he derives great physical pleasure.

In this novel Price also establishes Hutch as the central character of the trilogy, featuring him as the amalgam created and derived from several generations of complex genetic material. For those who have read *Surface, The Source of Light* provokes questions about Hutch's future which reflect upon four generations of forebears. One wonders whether Hutch will avoid the waste and recklessness which have handicapped his ancestors. One also wonders whether he will follow their path by marrying unwisely, bringing pain and suffering upon himself and others, or whether he will avoid a coupled life, turning instead to solitude and art, where he can memorialize and redeem his family's suffering. The novel generates questions reflecting upon Hutch and his heritage, yet—and to the disappointment of some readers—it then largely fails to provide answers, at least not until the third volume of the trilogy. Why?

As stated earlier, *The Source of Light* is less concerned with the long passage of time—what ultimately happens to people, how their lives unfold over decades—and more with how a young man passes through a critical stage in his life. At this point in time Hutch is confronted with a variety of antithetical yearnings: his central love for his father and yet his need to be free of him; his desire for others, both erotically and platonically, and yet his need for solitude and work; his desire for young men (Strawson Stuart, Lew Davis, James Nichols) and yet his need for a more conventional heterosexual marriage to Ann Gatlin. These are the central dilemmas in Hutch's life, and though the novel may disappoint some readers in not reaching any resolutions, Price has a different purpose in mind.

First, by leaving his narrative unresolved, Price may be demonstrating that the kind of permanent decision-making which society desires works against what is natural and human; as John Updike has said: "to be a person . . . is to be in a dialectical situation. A truly adjusted person is not a person at all."[25] Second, and more importantly, Price's concern is less with what ultimately happens to Hutch and more with how Rob and Hutch negotiate this crucial final ritual: the death of the father and the emergence of the son. Rob's death is in many ways the most important event in Hutch's life, and Price carefully explores how father and son prepare for and pass through this ordeal. Price also utilizes birth-related references and imagery to suggest that the novel is as much about birth as it is death. For both Rob and Hutch, Rob's death unfolds like a pregnancy and ensuing delivery—the actual time between the opening scene and Hutch's return to Europe is approximately nine months[26]—and at the moment of his death, Rob has a vision of his own birth from Eva's body. Shortly thereafter Hutch emerges from his old life, in which he was a son circling about his father, and finds himself born into his new existence as a free and independent man.

The title of the first section of the novel, "The Principle of Perturbations," is one of several astronomical terms which Price utilizes to organize and illuminate his novel. The term refers to a disturbance which upsets the normal rotation of two bodies around some center. Recall that in his poem for his father, Hutch describes himself and Rob as two orbiting bodies:

> What we had was years
> Of circling a spot, mules at a mill.
> The figure was rings, concentric rings
> Round an unseen center (what were we grinding?)
> Till I fled and you quit. (260)

The circularity of the Mayfield saga, seen in recurring family patterns and in the wedding ring itself, continues. Rob and Hutch, longtime companion bodies, have been circling together around some core—the center of earth? the source of rest?—but as it becomes apparent in the opening chapter, this mutual orbiting is ending. Rob's inoperable cancer, along with Hutch's departure for Europe, appear to be the perturbations which have upset their normal movement and rotation.

The novel begins in May of 1955 at Warm Springs, Virginia, where Rob and Hutch have met to share a curative bath before Hutch leaves for Europe. Springs have long been significant in Hutch's family: his paternal grandparents made their marital promises to one another at Panacea Springs, and his knowledge of his mother's family resonates with the spring at Goshen. In addition, underground springs are crucial, nearly holy places in Price's writing since they offer not only renewal and the hope of a cure (which Rob needs for his cancer and his wasteful life) but also a passage back to the core of the earth, the center of rest, the place toward which Price's characters yearn.

As one soon discovers, water imagery plays a significant role in the novel: Hutch assumes the "drowned-man act" when his father baptizes him; Rob learns he will essentially drown once his lungs fill with water, and his death comes in the form of a

A GREAT CIRCLE

"dense wave"; the spring water is described as female and womb-like; Archie Gibbons's father and sister have drowned in the sea. In this novel that is immersed in water imagery (*The Promise of Rest,* in contrast, will be concerned with fire and burning), water is associated with both birth and death. In addition, water acts as a crucial agent of separation. In Hutch's recurring dream, his mother, Rachel, stands on the opposite side of a creek, and by going abroad Hutch effectively separates himself from Rob, Ann, family, and home by water (the Atlantic Ocean).

Appropriately, this opening scene in the spring represents the beginning of a birth or rebirth for Hutch. In sharing the womb-like water with his father and in being given the right of baptism, Hutch is in the initial stage of a birth; later he will experience his dream of the tunnel—he "must dig for his life through a tunnel no bigger than his own clothed body" (17). As he writes in his poem to Rob the following January:

> . . . nine months ago, you and I in
> Warm Springs; the circular pool of fuming
> Water (female essence of the heart of the
> Ground) accepting your hard white limbs and
> Head in farewell grip more total than
> Any you'd known in air with prior
> Partners. (261)

Just as Hutch imagines himself in *Surface* as having emerged from Rob's body, literally Rob's groin, he also associates his rebirth, or his birth as a man independent of his father, with the body of Rob. This scene at the spring signals the conception of

Hutch's new life, into which he will be born with his father's death. For Hutch, whose own birth caused his mother's death, birth and death are always interrelated.

Another image Price introduces in this opening chapter is that of Hutch's rising. While his father baptizes him in the spring, Hutch resorts to the drowned-man act—"emptied his lungs so he fell to the smooth rocks that paved the spring"—then suddenly he "jerk[s] to life and thrust[s] toward the surface" where he breaks through and rises. This ritual between father and son signals Hutch's ascendancy, the fact that he will rise to assume his father's place. (Hutch actually rises from the water saying "Holy Ghost," recalling Jesus's baptism, in which the Holy Spirit descended upon him and identified him as the promised one— will Hutch thus be the promised one?)[27] In addition, Hutch—who is first seen naked before a mirror, examining that part of his groin which "bobbed in gratitude" when he "stroked the dim image"— is continually rising in an erotic sense throughout the novel, taking on a variety of male and female lovers. Finally, the image of the son's rising works in tandem with the incubus imagery which has played such a large role in the lives of Mayfield fathers and son. Hutch writes of how he "bore" Rob's weight, both literally when his father would lie upon him and figuratively through his father's troubles, yet the moment of Rob's death signals a dramatic change and a lightening of the load for Hutch, who suddenly finds himself raised.

After the opening chapters, in which Rob and Hutch part, the novel follows their lives in alternate fashion: Rob in North Carolina preparing for death, Hutch in Europe beginning his life away from Rob. Though Rob would like nothing more than his son's company during his final months, he refuses to tell Hutch of his illness, fearing it will destroy his son's European journey and, in effect, Hutch's chance to emerge from the burdens of his Mayfield past. Rob's sacrificial act is crucial since it allows Hutch to proceed with his plan and begin his act of separation and self-assertion.

As is apparent in the opening scene at the spring and generally throughout the novel, Rob and Hutch are extremely close. To some degree their relationship functions as a reverse or inverse oedipal attachment: instead of killing his father to be with his mother, Hutch has unknowingly "killed" his mother to be with his father. Yet despite their love and devotion for one another, Hutch has also been a source of "trouble" and responsibility for his father, and his father is currently the only obstacle in Hutch's path toward freedom. One of the true achievements of the novel is how Price frames the paradoxical nature of this union between father and son. In his memoir *Clear Pictures,* Price speaks of the "hard paradox" in his own father's death: though that death was devastating for Price, it was also liberating, enabling him as a young man "to move into that grown life I'd suddenly won."[28]

Although the most crucial and central love relationship in *The Source of Light* and in the entire trilogy is that between Rob and Hutch, they are precluded, at the very least by the boundaries of civilization, from any type of genital contact. Directly out of this prohibition arises one of the most interesting features of the novel: Hutch seeks in young men a surrogate for his father. In other words, he experiences his father sexually through the bodies of young men whom he encounters in his European travels. An apparent bisexual (though later he will express dissatisfaction with that term), Hutch seeks physical love not only in the body of his longtime lover, confidante, and apparent fiancée, Ann Gatlin, but also in attractive young men such as Strawson Stuart, Lew Davis, and James Nichols. These homosexual encounters, as Joyce Carol Oates points out, are of greater import and interest: "Hutch doesn't seem to grasp what the reader so quickly grasps—that his homosexual liaisons are much more meaningful to him."[29] Even forty years later in *The Promise of Rest,* Hutch does not appear fully to understand himself sexually, failing to see that young men are what he is primarily drawn to.

The young men answer to Hutch's need to know his father as a young man: "Hutch longed to see his father—not the Rob he had left three weeks ago but the grand lost boy who had lain beside him in infancy" (108). As Hutch sleeps with Strawson Stuart, a former student of his at the Episcopal Virginia boys' school, he is drawn closer to his father: "What [Hutch had] honored in this boy for nearly two years was the clear sight of life, a flood of cheerful animal life that had pressed Straw's body and face from within into one more mask of the thing Hutch hunted and worshiped in the world—the same strong grace that still moved the pictures of Rob through his memory" (144). And Hutch's attraction to James Nichols, the mason's helper and ex-convict, is directly linked to his father, who has since died: "something in the boy seemed identical with Rob, of the same good essence. Nothing ghostly or urgent but a gentle palpable return of the oldest presence he'd known and needed—the vulnerable potent needy youth who'd stood at the rim of Hutch's own childhood and asked for help" (309). Every lover who is of any value to Hutch is a mask of his father—an image that first appeared in Price's story "The Names and Faces of Heroes," in which Preacher's father's face serves as a mask for both the hero and Jesus. Through the relationship between Rob and Hutch, the reader encounters a significant truth: that love between a parent and child is often more stable, meaningful, and enduring than any other type of love, and that it is natural for such a love to generate erotic desire.

With this in mind, one begins to understand Price's use and depiction of other parent-child relations in the novel, such as that between James Nichols and his daughter, Nan, and the recently widowed Kay Gibbons and her son, Archie; they provide parallels for Rob and Hutch. Hutch sees himself in these other children, who are not only missing a parent (Nan's parents are separated; Archie's father is dead) but have been raised in troubled family circumstances. In addition, through James and Nan, who share a bed, travel together, and are essentially "in love," Price offers a direct parallel to Rob and Hutch: "Rob and himself twenty years ago, trailing through two states Rob's desperation and his own plain contentment to be with a father who could make old rocks in the road die laughing" (135). This scene of father and child together, in love and on the road, is archetypal in Price's fiction and includes Preacher and his father in "The Names and Faces of Heroes;" Tommy Ryden and his daughter, Lois Provo, in *A Generous Man;* Rob and Hutch in *The Surface of Earth;* and Paul Melton and his son, Logan, in *Private Contentment.* For Price this scene has powerful autobiographical roots; ten or more days a year he would get into a car with his traveling salesman father and experience what he describes as "wonderful, ideal days."[30]

The title of the second section of the novel, "The Rotation of Venus," is again an astronomical term. Its reference is to something that is obscure or mysterious: before 1961 Venus's rotation was unknown because the planet is shrouded in heavy clouds. Price chose the term because he liked its sound and because it offered a metaphor for another mystery in the novel: the complexity of Hutch's sexuality.[31] Around what sexual center—men, women, his father?—does Hutch rotate? As is evident in *The Promise of the Past,* this question remains pertinent throughout Hutch's life.

This second section of the novel focuses upon two events, the latter impinging upon the former: Hutch and Ann's rendez-vous in Rome for Christmas, and Hutch's return to North Caro-lina for his father's death. Price's Rome resonates not only with the palpability of the past, its layers of history and ruins, but also—particularly because of the time of the year—with the presence of the Child, the Christ Child. Hutch and Ann, in fact, witness a mass in which "promised fragments of the only Man-ger" are displayed; the scene itself then "pressed from each of them their unknown will to start a child" (162). Yet this will not be the new Messiah. In contrast to the glorious birth of Christ, Hutch and Ann's child will be aborted—another birth and death connection in the novel. The visit to Rome ends disastrously. Almost immediately after he sires his first child, Hutch leaves Ann in Rome to be with his dying father in North Carolina. Lonely and hurt, Ann sleeps with a young American soldier named Rowlet Swanson. Though Hutch has given the Mayfield family ring to Ann in Rome, there is every indication that their relationship is ending.

The central event in this section, and in the novel as a whole, is Rob's death; few scenes in Price are more powerful. With Hutch in the hospital, holding Rob's wrist and feeling the final pulse, Rob climbs into "his own free flight" and sees himself entering an old dark house. He proceeds through every room, bearing a "peaceful confidence the house had a center which it somehow served in total silence" (209–10). At last he is led to a light and enters a room where he finds a sixteen- or seventeen-year-old girl on the bed-sheets delivering a child, whom she then places on her breast. Rob appears at last to have reached his center of rest and "source of light": "His mother, himself, the room he is born in. Feasible center, discovered in time, revised now and right" (210). With Rob's death comes birth, not only for himself (his literal birth from Eva's womb) but also for Hutch: "The same dense wave that had drowned his father spread up through his hand and raised him higher than he'd been this whole day of hope" (210).

For Hutch, the anticipation of Rob's death is paradoxical in nature: there is "a deep relief that Rob was going and yielding him room" and yet "a deeper fear that the room would be vacant, containing no center round which he could move in the confident swings he'd learned from birth" (199). Once Rob is gone, Hutch feels "lighter" than ever, yet he also experiences "Rob's absence fully for the first time" and realizes that there cannot be another center, another fixed single point for him to revolve around (241). Though Rob's ghost makes a return visit, Hutch will be forced to draw upon some other form of motion in his life ahead.

The title of the third section of the novel, "The Center of Gravity," applies directly to Hutch's new situation: now that his father has died, what will be his new center of gravity? It does not appear that any one person can take Rob's place as his center, and Hutch does not feel the need or hunger for a single and constant companion: "He thought that such a need must be taught, almost surely by a mother," and since his mother died at his birth, he has not experienced it (91). In addition, the stories from literature which provide a subtext to the novel—*Tristan and Iseult, Macbeth,* King Arthur—suggest the inevitable failure of marriage, and one suspects, though wrongly as it turns out, that Hutch and Ann will not marry.

There are, of course, other possibilities and hopes for Hutch's future. In his poem Hutch tells his deceased father, "I will have your life, / The life you hunted but never caught" (260). One senses that Hutch is not at the raw mercy of his emotions in the way his father was, and that he will be able to live a less painful, more productive life than Rob. Related to this is the strong possibility that Hutch will use his life to discover and develop those artistic skills which will redeem him and his family, that he will "fulfill his father's request that all of their domestic suffering be converted into something meaningful," and that the story of those past generations of their family will be made into a useful "diagram."[32] In fact, while reading Bedier's *Tristan and Iseult,* Hutch identifies with Gorvenal, Tristan's loyal servant who provides patient witness to the tragedy of others; perhaps this will be Hutch's role.

Though the reader is offered no solid clue as to Hutch's future, Price ends with a surprising remark by Polly Drewry in a letter to Hutch: "All the men in your family were happy men. Not one of them knew it till I said so. I have said it to you and I know I'm right" (318). Polly's statement adds to the novel's irresolution and provokes central questions about the Mayfield men and Hutch, such as whether their lives have been full of suffering and waste, as suspected, or whether they have been "happy" lives, as Polly suggests (and are the two necessarily contradictory?). Similarly, one wonders how much Hutch resembles his Mayfield forebears. Polly forces the reader to reassess the lives of the Mayfield men, and though she is not entirely convincing, due to her own self-interest in having cared for and shared in the lives of these men, she seems accurate in her assessment of Hutch. On the verge of a new life as an artist, free at last of familial entanglements, and initiated into fulfilling erotic encounters, Hutch is alive and happy. Yet as the reader will see in *The Promise of Rest,* this state of mind cannot last forever.

The Promise of Rest

Though *The Promise of Rest* continues an earlier story, it is in some ways a departure for Price. First, the novel takes place in 1993, one of the rare Price novels and the only volume from the trilogy to be set in, and at the same time actively explore, a contemporary world. *The Promise of Rest* is, among other things, Price's AIDS novel, as one finds the Mayfield family, with their history of erotic hunger, suddenly living in an era in which love can kill. Second, *The Promise of Rest* is far more candid and aggressive in addressing questions concerning race. Price's cast of black characters in *Promise* is more diverse than in his other novels, and Wyatt Bondurant, Price's first semi-militant black, forces one to reassess the Mayfields in regard to racism, particularly their treatment of kinsman Grainger Walters. Finally, *Promise* more openly confronts issues of sexuality, particularly homosexuality, which becomes the dominant and preferred form of coupling in the novel. Though a few of Price's characters in earlier works have homosexual experiences or tendencies, very little is explicitly stated there.

The Promise of Rest picks up the story found in *The Source of Light,* though there is a leap forward of thirty seven years in the time setting, from 1956 to 1993. Hutch Mayfield suddenly is a man of sixty-two, with a son seven years older than Hutch himself was at the end of the prior novel. Price, though, spends relatively little time filling in the gaps. Instead, and as with *The Source of Light,* his focus is on the present, four months during the spring and summer of 1993, and specifically on how a father and son negotiate a difficult passage in the present. Also once again, death figures as the central event with which father and son must cope; only this time, Hutch will be dealing with the death of his son.

The Promise of Rest answers questions which *The Source of Light* leaves unresolved. As one might expect, Hutch becomes an artist, a well-known poet, and returns to North Carolina, teaching at Duke University like Price himself. In addition, Hutch has married Ann Gatlin. Though the possibility of marriage to Ann is distinct in *The Source of Light,* by the end of the novel it appears such a marriage is doomed because of Hutch's need both for solitude and young men—a situation the reader seemingly understands better than Hutch. It is no surprise then that Hutch and Ann have separated; one, in fact, wonders how they ever managed to stay together for more than thirty-five years.

Despite the progress of Hutch's life and career, many of the same unresolved problems and questions from the earlier novel persist in *The Promise of Rest.* For instance, Hutch's sexuality continues to be a mystery, and one wonders whether he has

A GREAT CIRCLE

deceived himself his entire life by having chosen a woman over a man. In addition, questions concerning race persist, such as whether Hutch's care of Grainger demonstrates devoted love or racist guilt, or some combination. Finally, there are continuing mysteries regarding Hutch's relationship to his ancestors. One wonders whether Hutch has been able to depart from the behavior of his male ancestors and avoid their wasteful patterns, and whether he, or any Mayfield for that matter, has been able to realize a sense of rest. These are the significant questions of the novel, though not a single one can be answered definitively as Price again maintains a splendid sense of irresolution.

Like both *The Source of Light* and *The Surface of Earth, The Promise of Rest* begins in the spring, a time of renewal, and no one is more in need of renewal than Hutch. Bitterly separated from both his wife and dying son, Hutch is alone and ostensibly dead at the beginning of the novel; as he tells a student, "I'm alone as a dead tree."[33] Having lost the people he most loves, primarily through his own distance and self- absorption, he has forgotten what it means to have a live body; in essence he has become "a cold engine," a "frozen" man. The aspiring artist who craved solitude in *The Source of Light* has succeeded in shutting himself off from the rest of the world, and now he is miserable. Yet, as one sees in the opening classroom scene at Duke, a mysterious change is beginning to take place in Hutch: "suddenly [he] felt a surge of pleasure—a strange boiling from deep in his chest" (8); and by the end of the class, in which he has covered Milton's "Lycidas" and spoken confessionally about the coming death of his own son, Hutch wonders, "*What in God's name has got me happy?*" (12).

It is difficult to pinpoint a single answer to this mystery because Price offers so many: it is spring; Hutch feels useful when teaching; no words please him more than Milton's "Lycidas"; he is thrilled to be able to crown Milton the supreme poet; it relieves him to have confessed to his students about his son's illness; he is looking forward to Grainger's birthday; he may even be experiencing a clairvoyant pleasure in restoring contact with his son. Throughout the novel Price will continue to offer reasonable explanations for Hutch's growing sense of elation: Wyatt has died; Hutch begins taking primary possession of his son's death; Hutch is getting back at Ann by "walling her out" of Wade's death. Though all of these explanations seem reasonable and accurate, not a single one can account for Price's suggestion that Hutch somehow "loves" his "son's pain and death" (119). How in the world can this be, particularly for a father who loves his son more than anything?

The best approach toward understanding Hutch's attitude is again through the unusual circumstances of his birth. Because his mother died in giving him life, Hutch sees an inextricable connection between birth and death—with one comes the other. As horrible as Wade's death is for Hutch, it also signals his own resuscitation. From the opening scene forward, Hutch is waking up, returning to life; even his sexual energy will eventually be restored. The man who had put a "freeze" on his dealings with his wife and son is again becoming human. Thus one finds one of the strangest and yet most original messages in all of Price's fiction: from the devastating death of a child there can come rebirth, even elation. Price's epigraph from Eliot's "Little Gidding" may help to explain:

A GREAT CIRCLE

> We die with the dying:
> See, they depart, and we go with them.
> We are born with the dead:
> See, they return, and bring us with them.

Throughout the novel and the entire trilogy, there are both loss and gain in death. Hutch loses a part of himself both literally and figuratively with his son's death, yet he also achieves significant gains: renewed contact with loved ones; news of the possibility of a grandson, Raven Bondurant; the continued hope of an afterlife, "the promise of rest"; and the birth of a new poem.

Price's opening classroom scene serves purposes beyond the revelation of Hutch's incipient feelings of elation. First, it sets the tone for the novel. Hutch's recital and discussion of "Lycidas" lends an elegiac tone and foreshadows several events: the coming death and hopeful rest of Wade Mayfield (whereas Milton's Edward King experienced death by water, Wade will be the victim of fire—passion, AIDS, cremation); and the grief and mourning which Hutch will suffer (one wonders whether he too will need to compose a poem about a young man's death).

Second, the reading of "Lycidas" demonstrates the significance and power of words for Hutch. In a novel offering a mini-anthology of English poetry—poems by Milton, Keats, Blake, Bishop, Shakespeare, Eliot, and by fictional characters such as Hart Salter, Maitland Moses, and Hutch—one sees just how much poetry matters to Hutch and how it aids his survival. As he states: "This poem—'Lycidas'—means more to me than all but a few of the humans I've known. . . . If the world hadn't turned up creatures like Milton . . . I doubt I could live through the thought of my young son dying in pain" (12). In fact, one sometimes wonders whether Hutch is moved more by poetry than by people.

Finally, the opening scene frames two significant questions concerning the artistic process. Does art necessarily come from authentic and "sincere" emotions? Can an old familiar theme be written again? Price's answer to each appears to be yes. The former, the authenticity question, applies to Hutch's present state of mind and concerns whether he will be able to compose a poem from the devastating and painful death of Wade. The latter, the originality question, concerns whether yet another story about Anglo- and African-American miscegenation can be written. Since Hutch's answer is the one a writer must give—yes, so long as he "takes it up in flaming-new language"—one is led to believe that Price uses this opening scene to anticipate and thus to defuse a familiar criticism: that he is merely recycling Faulkner and other southern literature. Price's treatment of miscegenation will prove to be different from Faulkner's. In Price there is not only passion, hostility, and discomfort between white and black but also care, love, and sensitivity. As Hutch says, "the problem [of miscegenation] has gone much further toward both solution and utter insolubility than Marse Will Faulkner ever dreamed possible" (11). The partnership between Wyatt Bondurant and Wade Mayfield bodes well for any hope of mutuality, yet Wyatt's attitude toward Hutch conversely points to the near impossibility of any solution. In whichever direction racial relations go—toward reconciliation or further hostility—Price suggests that the future of the Mayfield line and of America will be one of increasingly mixed racial blood.

A GREAT CIRCLE

As with the earlier novels of the trilogy, *The Promise of Rest* quickly moves to a father-son reunion and an ensuing period of time in which father and son strive to find a shared peace. What is different about the reunion in *The Promise of Rest* is that it occurs almost entirely through the efforts of others. At Grainger's birthday party, Grainger, Straw, and Emily virtually conspire to lead Hutch to New York City and return home with Wade. Though Wade is the "only human [Hutch has] loved with no real reservation since his father died," Hutch is frozen with bitterness and resentment toward his son and is hardly ready to proceed on his own. Recall that Wade has not only fallen in love with a man who despises Hutch, but he has abandoned his father, refusing even to inform him of his illness and impending death.

Certainly Hutch's instinct toward distance is a factor in this split between father and son, yet race and sexuality, the two major issues in the novel, play a more central role. Wade Mayfield has chosen an African-American homosexual as his partner. The embodiment of what both white and heterosexual America fear, Wyatt has been "the main obstruction," the "all but impassable wall between Hutch and Wade" (40). Race is primarily what causes the tension between Wyatt and Hutch, and thus between Wade and Hutch. Wyatt despises the Mayfields, who he believes see him as "the field hand buck that had ravished their darling," and he refers to Wade's family as "Murder Incorporated" (157–58). Though Wyatt's remarks are extreme and unfair, he offers truths which trouble Hutch, such as how Hutch can allow his kinsman Grainger to live a separate and unequal existence as a "house pet" and "tame crippled monkey." Through his "quiet assent," Hutch has allowed the "unstopped crime" of racism to continue. Wade, on the other hand, is the first Mayfield truly to break the color barrier, committing himself for life and death to a black man. There is an element of sacrifice in Wade's relationship with Wyatt; out of love, and perhaps out of a need to redeem the wrongs of his kin, Wade relinquishes his relationship with his father and, finally, his life itself. Through Wade and Wyatt—both of whom are sacrificed in the process—the longtime though secretive attraction between white Mayfields and black men and women is at last cast into the light of day.

As for the issue of sexuality, Wyatt believes Hutch condemns the way he and Wade choose to live. Though Hutch is open-minded and liberal enough to prove Wyatt mostly wrong, one wonders how much Hutch's confusion about his own sexual orientation colors his feelings toward Wade and Wyatt. The two young men are able to experience what Hutch was not bold or passionate enough to choose, and one wonders whether he is envious and resentful. There also exists the possibility that Hutch may be angry at Wade for living a homosexual life, which has led to his contracting the AIDS virus, or even angry at himself both for giving Wade the genes that essentially cause his death and for not having spoken more frankly to his son about his own homosexual inclinations. Though Price does not provide easy answers, one discovers something new through the character of Wade. He is the first Mayfield to openly acknowledge and pursue, without guilt, shame, or fear, the two desires which so many of his ancestors have repressed or experienced only furtively: an attraction to blacks and to other men. By living openly and equally with a black homosexual, Wade bridges the racial and sexual gaps which have stymied his father.

A GREAT CIRCLE

As stated earlier, *The Promise of Rest* is the Price novel most eager to confront issues of race and sexuality. Most of the major characters are, to use Hutch's term of preference, either full- or part-time "queers": Hutch, Straw, Wade, Wyatt, Alice Matthews, Maitland Moses, Jimmy Boat, and Cam Mapleson. One of Price's purposes, it would appear, is to dispel myths and ignorance about homosexual behavior. For instance, through Ann's condemnation of Wade's "choice" of homosexuality, Price tries to disarm the argument that one *chooses* one's sexuality; even though Hutch chooses to live with a woman instead of a man, Price would seemingly argue that Hutch does not have a choice about his attraction to men. Another myth Price attempts to debunk is that homosexual men are more promiscuously inclined than heterosexual men. Not only does Wade swear he has had only two male lovers in his lifetime, but he tells Mait, "If straight men weren't hardwired for women, with all women's training and doubts and plumbing problems, they'd fuck as many times a day as the most crazed queer" (182). Among other things, *The Promise of Rest* serves to legitimize and normalize homosexuality.

Questions about homosexuality become even more pertinent in the novel because they apply directly to Hutch, who alternately assumes the role of expert in response to Mait's and Jimmy's questions about homosexuality and that of the unknowing initiate to Straw's understanding of what Hutch has denied in himself. Though Hutch is unapologetic and candid about his homosexual past, he appears to have denied that aspect of his erotic life for nearly forty years. His explanation for this denial— that no household can exist for long without children and with two "male-thinking minds"—is not entirely convincing. In fact, later in the novel Hutch begins to "hear Straw's voice speaking through him, edging him off his old objections" (244). Though Hutch's sexuality remains a mystery, it appears that, as is the case in *The Source of Light,* his primary attraction is toward men. During this period of intense grief and loneliness, Hutch now turns almost exclusively to young and attractive men for comfort: Straw, Mait, Jimmy, and Hart.

In addition, it appears Hutch and Straw missed a great opportunity nearly forty years earlier because of Hutch's timidity, confusion, and stinginess. Had they stayed together, Hutch argues, they would have destroyed each other; yet Straw counters, "What would have been worse than you killing me or vice versa?" (54). Straw's question sets up a splendid parallel with Wade and Wyatt, who actually do kill one another, and thus leads the reader to question which is better: to die in a figurative sense from loneliness and self-isolation like Hutch, or to die literally through passion and "burning" as Wade and Wyatt do. Though Price does not necessarily endorse one way or the other, one senses that living "throttle out" is preferable to a life of solitude and emotional death.

All this, of course, leads to Price's depiction of AIDS, which must stand as one of the more powerful and convincing representations of a catastrophic illness in contemporary fiction. Through its "burning" and "flaming" imagery, AIDS provides the appropriate terminus to a trilogy chronicling how a line of men in a single family have fueled themselves on love and passion, effectively consuming themselves in the process. Despite the fact that Wade's body is "burned up" by AIDS, and finally cremated so that he is mere ashes at the novel's close, Price finds beauty in Wade's "flaming" existence. Whereas earlier generations of Mayfields burned in waste and recklessness, Wade burns in love. One senses in *Promise* an adjustment in Price's philosophy: waste, which has earlier been associated with passion and hunger, now has more to do with stinginess, self-absorption, and coldness, as embodied in Hutch. Whereas the earlier two novels of the trilogy are more supportive of independence and solitude, particularly for the artist, *The Promise of Rest* emphasizes the need for love, touch, and the presence of others.

In his handling of the novel's imagery, Price associates "burning" with living and continually refers to bodies being like "fire" and giving off "light": Cam's body "flare[s] like a phosphorus fire"; Wade's grin produces "the strongest afterglow"; Straw is a "*lightning rod*" possessing "ravenous heat"; Grainger's life "burned on . . . [and] gave off its strength like a tangible radiance" (171, 165, 232, 130). In addition one sees, through the deteriorated vision of Wade, human beings taking on the appearance of streaks of light. In *The Promise of Rest,* heat and fire is life: a sexually charged individual like Straw is on fire; great poetry demands a "flaming-new language"; and body heat is literally necessary to prolong life. Wyatt and Wade burn in love, and then their passion literally consumes their bodies through the ravenous appetite of AIDS, yet Price hardly condemns their behavior. Instead the novel endorses sexuality, albeit expressed through safe sexual practices, as Wade's advice to Mait, and presumably to Hutch, is: "Don't hoard your body" (196). Stinginess, Hutch's primary failing, is, according to Wade, "as mean a failing as anything else but strangling children" (196).

The burning imagery also pertains to race. Price writes of history as "a permanent bonfire," sacrificial in nature, in which "black people have burned" (256). Through events such as the recent L.A. riots and references to black men "coming with sickles," Price suggests the future may indeed be a racial bonfire—a concept that relates to the theme of America's demise. In an unusual narrative move, Price allows his characters to drive north of the Mason-Dixon line and enter a large, contemporary northern city, where he proceeds to demonstrate just how America has been "botched." Beyond the roaring fires of AIDS and racial tension, America has deteriorated physically—the filth and destroyed landscape of New Jersey and New York City—and intellectually: Americans can no longer write and instead spend most of their time watching TV. In *The Promise of Rest* Price suggests as bleak and as doomed a future for America as one finds in any of his novels since *Love and Work.*

Yet, as in all of Price's work, there is hope, and it resides in several places. One source is the continuing line of black angels or saints who populate *A Great Circle:* Grainger Walters, Jimmy Boat, Ivory Bondurant. Another is the "secret child," whose identity does not become fully clear until late in the novel. Though the characters are not certain of Raven's paternity, Price's narrator reveals that Raven Patterson Bondurant is Wade's son and that Wade's traits will seep into Raven through the Stuart cavalier doll which Hutch gives the young man. A mixture of Mayfield, Patterson, and Bondurant blood, Raven is the culmination of nearly a century of kindness between the Mayfields and Pattersons, and as a vessel of mixed races, he represents the future of black-white relations: continuing hostility, or reconciliation and mutuality.

A GREAT CIRCLE

Of course the greatest hope, as the title suggests, is in "the promise of rest." Price's recurring use of the word *promise* creates an echo as characters continually ask one another for "promises": to love, to be faithful, to return, to remember, and finally to rest. Wade, in fact, makes his parents "promise" they will not keep him alive artificially, that they will allow him to rest. It appears that Wade ultimately earns his "rest," for at the moment of his death he is greeted by his deceased grandfather, Rob Mayfield, who pulls him into the blinding light. Though Wade's life has been shorter than the lives of any of his male ancestors, his has also burned brighter, and through his consummation of a powerful and mutual love which even his parents cannot destroy, he in some sense has ended the Mayfield demon or curse.

CHAPTER FOUR

Artists and Outlaws

The remaining Price novels not dealing with the Mustian or Mayfield families conveniently fit into either one of two categories defining the protagonist: artist or outlaw. *Love and Work* (1968) and *The Tongues of Angels* (1990) are, among other things, *künstlerromans*—portraits of artists. The former is a rather cerebral rendering of the novelist Thomas Eborn, and the latter, told from the point of view of the realist landscape painter Bridge Boatner, is an artist's initiation story. Though Price has been narrowly and even pejoratively categorized as the author of untutored, working-class rurals, much of his work actually deals with highly intelligent, psychologically sophisticated artists. In both of these novels—as in *The Source of Light, The Promise of Rest, Permanent Errors,* and *Clear Pictures*—Price centrally explores the world of the artist and his work.

The other familiar Price protagonist is the outlaw, a label Price uses to describe such characters as Kate Vaiden, Blue Calhoun, and Wesley Beavers. For Price these characters are not hardened criminals but individuals "who would not be approved of by the official judgmental bodies of our culture (the churches, the courts and so forth)": "They're outlaws, they're not officially acceptable people. But I think they're profoundly good people."[1] Price's emotional or moral outlaws do not murder or rob but instead are more likely to abandon lovers, spouses, or children—sometimes in order to satisfy an impulse or relieve a pressure, other times for reasons mostly mysterious. Though their behavior is occasionally reckless or selfish, Price's outlaws are basically thoughtful, considerate people who at some point simply refuse to continue to live in the style prescribed by society. Two of Price's most successful novels in regard to book sales, *Kate Vaiden* (1986) and *Blue Calhoun* (1992), revolve around outlaw protagonists, and the financial success of these novels indicates the truth of Price's judgment that "everybody likes outlaws better than they like churchgoers."[2]

Kate Vaiden

Published in 1986, *Kate Vaiden* was the most critically acclaimed of Price's novels since *A Long and Happy Life.* Receiving both critical and popular accolades, the novel won the National Book Critics Circle Award and was deemed Price's most accessible work in at least two decades. The primary explanation for the novel's success was its voice. As Rosellen Brown wrote in her front-page review in the *New York Times Book Review,* "the voice of Mr. Price's heroine blows like fresh air across the page."[3]

Kate Vaiden is Price's first novel to be written in the first person and his first since *A Long and Happy Life* to be centrally engaged with a female character, a fact suggesting that narrative from a female perspective is a particular strength of his.[4] One hears a far more inviting, appealing, forgiving, and spirited voice in *Kate Vaiden* than one hears in the omniscient narrator of Price's preceding three novels, *Love and Work, The Surface of Earth,* and *The Source of Light.* In those novels, which character- ize his work from the late 1960s through the early 1980s, Price speaks in a voice which can be austere, solemn, detached, and at times even biblical or oracular in nature.

Due to the appeal and acclaim of *Kate Vaiden,* one is inclined toward two conclusions: it is Price's best novel, and it signals a reclaiming of that more colloquial and exuberant prose style found in his earliest fiction, a style which comes closest to capturing Price's natural or best voice. One may even support these conclusions by pointing to the fact that after the success of *Kate Vaiden,* Price steers away from omniscient, austere narration toward a more colloquial first-person approach: two of his next three novels, as well as parts of the third, are written in the first person, and in much of his recent nonfiction work, Price turns to more personal modes of writing. Though Price's recent work has benefited from this more personal approach, the above conclusions are problematic. First, though *Kate Vaiden* is a good novel, it is not Price's best. It lacks the panoramic scope and genealogical weight of *The Surface of Earth* and the poetic richness of *A Long and Happy Life.* Second, though the voice in *Kate Vaiden* is more inviting and accessible than those voices found in certain other Price novels, it is not a qualitatively better or truer voice.

Just as readers find Kate's voice to be powerful and engaging, so do characters in the novel. Douglas Lee, the father of Kate's child, answers Kate's question "What's so grand about me . . . ?" by stating: "Your voice. . . . You could talk your way through granite rock."[5] Like so many of Price's characters, Kate is a wonderful talker, yet in light of her present objective, it is imperative that she be. The novel, after all, is more than a recounting of the events of her life; it is, Price has said, "her apologia for her particular existence," her confession in which she must explain and justify her life to herself, her son, and the reader. As Price has further explained, "She's writing the story down, a) to find out if she has the right to tell it to [her son, whom she abandoned forty years prior] and, b) to have something to tell him once she does indeed decide whether she's going to locate him or not."[6] Thus her words may play a crucial role in deciding her future: a potential reunion with her son hangs in the balance.

Kate's telling arouses several questions with regard to the reader. First, does she make the reader understand, even sympathize with, her seemingly reprehensible act of abandoning her child? Second, how reliable is she; does one believe all she says? And third, does the reader believe that Price, a male, has successfully created the voice of a woman? The answer to the first question is yes. Though one may not fully understand or agree with Kate's decision to abandon her son, one sympathizes with her and comes to understand how her orphaned history and damaged past have made her unusually fearful of and resistant to human attachments. As for the second question—is Kate fully reliable?—the answer is probably no. Arguing that "Kate's family is riven by buried secrets and by infidelities hastily exorcised by piles of poor lies," Joseph Dewey suggests Kate's language is "debased and counterfeit" and "never a vehicle for honest confession or humane engagement."[7] Though Kate's unreliability may be less extreme than Dewey suggests, narrative accountability is nevertheless in question. In telling her story, Kate is not only working from distant memories she has never fully understood, but her narrative strategy is to demonstrate to and convince her son that despite her flaws and sins, she is worth knowing and forgiving. In addition, one wonders whether Kate's work as a stenographer—taking down the stories of others, particularly criminals—affects the way in which she tells her story.

Finally, for the third question, concerning Price's ability to write a reverse gender novel, one needs to consider background material. Several months after *Kate Vaiden* appeared, Price published an essay entitled "A Vast Common Room," which argues, among other things, that men and women share "total human sympathy" and are thus mutually capable of knowing and creating characters and voices of the other's gender.[8] The essay disputes the sometimes feminist notion that a man cannot understand or write from the perspective of a woman, and vice versa, and it encourages writers to work across gender lines as Price has with *Kate Vaiden.*

As to whether Price succeeds in his reverse gender effort, Rosellen Brown writes: "Mr. Price's successful creation of a female voice may be a tour de force, but it never feels like a showy ventriloquial act. Instead, Kate is a wholly convincing girl and a not improbable woman."[9] Many other critics, male and female— Michiko Kakutani, Jefferson Humphries, Elaine Kendall, Robert Towers, and the large majority of the novel's reviewers—agree that Kate is credible. Yet Edith Hartin finds Kate's voice to be "completely the product of a masculine imagination, a masculine tradition," which "sounds more like a man's fantasy than a woman's experience." Hartin condemns Price for creating a stereotypical and unsympathetic woman who is passive, irresponsible, and contemptuous of other women, and she concludes that "while Price, the self-proclaimed female impersonator, can sing in a cool soprano, many readers remain aware that all he must do is clear his throat to resume a resounding baritone."[10]

Though her argument is not convincing—it has less to do with Kate's believability as a woman and more perhaps with Kate's not being the kind of woman Hartin would like her to be— Hartin nevertheless forces the reader to consider a crucial dimension of the novel: has Price truly pulled off being a woman? What seems particularly compelling is that the overwhelming majority of female reviewers find Kate to be convincing in a novel which confronts what Dewey calls the "signal moments in female development": menstruation, early sexual experience, pregnancy, labor and delivery, motherhood, and menopause.[11] Certainly a less than credible narrator could never have successfully negotiated these moments.

The plot of *Kate Vaiden* is fairly complex and episodic in structure, with Kate running to and then away from family and friends throughout North Carolina and Virginia towns—Greensboro, Raleigh, Macon, Norfolk, Franklin, and Asheville. Though the novel begins in 1984, with the fifty-seven- year-old Kate recovering from cancer surgery and trying to decide whether she can tell her story to her son, Lee Vaiden, Price pays little attention to the present. The story is primarily concerned with Kate's adolescent years, from the time she is eleven until she is approximately eighteen; thus the majority of the book takes place between 1938 and 1945, the war years. Price devotes only about forty pages to the next forty years of Kate's life, from 1945 to 1984, suggesting the crucial moments for Kate all came during adolescence.

The most crucial moment, of course, is her father Dan's murder of her mother, Frances, and his subsequent suicide; this is the primal event which shapes the rest of Kate's life. An eleven-year-old orphan, Kate is taken in by her Aunt Caroline, Uncle Holt, and their black servant, Noony, who all live in the small town of Macon, North Carolina. Though Kate is given a good life in Macon by these kind and saintly surrogate parents, she is not content to remain there, or anywhere, for very long.

Much of her adolescent life, in Macon and other towns, is spent in the company of men, most of whom are a good deal older than Kate: Fob Foster, a middle-aged bachelor cousin in Macon who teaches her to ride a horse; Gaston Stegall, a slightly older boy who initiates her to the mysteries of sexuality and love; Walter Porter, a homosexual cousin living in Norfolk who welcomes her when she runs away from Caroline; Douglas Lee, a fellow orphan who is prone toward violent behavior and who fathers Kate's child; Tim Slaughter, a cab driver who offers his services as a shining knight of rescue; and Whitfield Eller, a blind piano tuner for whom Kate works as a chauffeur. Kate, though, does not remain with any of these men for long, fleeing each domestic or romantic situation when it threatens to become more permanent.By the time she is eighteen, Kate has experienced more tragedy and pain than most endure in a lifetime: her mother's murder, her father's suicide, and the apparent suicides of the two men whom she has loved (Douglas and Gaston). In addition, she has given birth to, and then abandoned, an illegitimate son. At this point, with these horrendous events behind her, Kate ostensibly quits life. Like Milo Mustian in *A Generous Man,* Kate is overwhelmed by a dramatic and intense adolescence, an experience which leads her to withdraw from the world: "My life stopped there, my old life as Kate.... I gradually vanished" (259). As is often the case in Price's work, adulthood brings resignation and conformity, crushing the exuberant possibilities of adolescence. For Kate, the vanishing act lasts nearly forty years, but then circumstances arise—a bout with cervical cancer and a revelatory visit to St. Peter's Cathedral in Rome, home to "the biggest quitter in human history"—which lead her to compose her story and consider whether she has the right to see her abandoned son.

Kate Vaiden is Price's "orphan novel," written in part to investigate and imagine the life of his own mother, an orphan raised by an elder sister in Macon. Though it is by no means a strict accounting of his mother's life, Price calls the novel "a credible expression of my mother's own spiritual potential."[12] The novel is filled with orphans; in addition to Kate, there are Frances Vaiden, Kate's mother; Douglas Lee, Kate's lover and the father to her child; Lee Vaiden, Kate's son; and perhaps even Whitfield Eller. Aunt Caroline, in fact, raises three successive generations of orphans: Frances, Kate, and Lee.

As one discovers through Kate, the central fact shaping and influencing every subsequent relationship in her life is her orphan childhood. Such a childhood, as the novel demonstrates, can cause tremendous damage: Douglas emerges as an angry, violent, and resentful man who takes his own life, and Kate develops into a woman unusually fearful of commitment and attachment. In addition, Kate appears to feel both guilty for having caused her parents' problems and deaths, and incompetent for having been unable to hold on to her parents. The result is a rather bleak and lonely future; the fate of an orphan, Price suggests, is either to continue being orphaned in subsequent relationships, or to orphan others. Kate opts for the latter; as she says, "*Leave people before they can plan to leave you*" (179).

Kate's orphaned past helps the reader understand what is, on the surface, so shocking in the novel: her abandonment of her own child. As Kate writes, "Fathers can walk out on whole nests of children every day of the year and never return, never send back a dime—that's considered sad but natural. But an outlaw mother is the black last nightmare any man can face" (282). Price agrees that society adheres to this double standard and adds, "We are still horrified by the mother who really says, 'I don't want these children.'"[13] As he often does, Price creates a character whose actions are seemingly immoral, perhaps abnormal, maybe even unforgivable, and then he leads the reader, through the voice of that character, to the point from which one can begin to understand and empathize. In the case of Kate Vaiden, Price demonstrates that there are women who do not "accept the great mother stereotype," are not totally devoted to their children, and yet are not horrible people.[14]

As to why Kate abandons her son, there are several possible answers. First, she sees herself as a dangerous woman, a killer of men (Dan, Gaston, Douglas), a Jonah who brings disaster on those she loves; and she fears she will do the same to Lee: "I'd caused the death of every man that touched me, really *touched* me in need. . . . Could I kill [Lee] too?" (257). A second possibility is that she fears she will be a bad role model for Lee and that he is in healthier hands with Caroline. Each of these possibilities suggests that she abandons Lee to save him; thus, the paradox:

she saves Lee by making him an orphan. Of course, another possibility is that Kate's reasons are more selfish, that she leaves Lee for the same reason she apparently leaves everyone else: she fears she will lose him or that he will leave her first. All of these explanations make Kate more likeable, yet a final possibility is that she simply is not interested in devoting her life to the care of a child; as she says, "*I did not want him*" (264). This is no doubt the hardest explanation for many readers to swallow, and it is made even more difficult by the fact that Kate never appears to feel shame for her actions.

Blue Calhoun

In many respects *Blue Calhoun* stands as a companion novel to *Kate Vaiden.*[15] Both are first-person, eponymous narratives, largely confessional in tone, in which the speaker, a moral outlaw of sorts, offers an accounting of his or her life and of how it went wrong. Both novels are also written ostensibly to or for a single reader—Kate's son, Lee, in *Kate Vaiden,* and Blue's granddaughter, Lyn, in *Blue Calhoun*—who has been harmed by the speaker's past actions and who remains the crucial person to render judgment upon and grant mercy to the speaker. In addition, both novels employ a similar structure and pacing, with the speakers in both works spending the bulk of the pages examining a significant year or span of several years in the long-ago past (1938–1945 in *Kate Vaiden,* and 1956–1957 in *Blue Calhoun*), devoting the final fifty or so pages of their narratives to bringing the reader up to date on the most recent thirty or forty years of their lives, and ending at a slightly ambiguous juncture—where one can only guess as to the reaction of the speaker's intended reader. Finally, both novels offer a protagonist who is surrounded by members of the opposite sex. Blue tells us flatly that "From the day I was born, I'd . . . been a soul that loves women," and most of his emotional energy is now channeled toward the many women who inspire, frustrate, and share in his life: his wife, Myra; his daughter, Mattie; his mother, Miss Ashlyn; his lover, Luna; and his granddaughter, Lyn.

Beyond these structural resemblances, both novels were greeted with extraordinary popular praise and enthusiasm, more than almost any of Price's other novels—a reception due largely, it seems, to the fluidity, grace, lyricism, and vitality of the first-person narrators. What is so overwhelmingly appealing and striking about *Blue Calhoun* in particular is its narrative voice, which has led reviewers to call the novel "wonderfully lyrical," "near operatic," "rhythmic and exact, almost psalmodic," and "like a spin through a cool tunnel of leafy spring trees."[16] Several reviewers, largely on the basis of Blue's narration, rated *Blue Calhoun* as Price's best novel or among his best, an evaluation perhaps bolstered by the novel's selling more copies in hardcover than any other Price novel to date. One should be aware, though, that the novel's reception was not unanimously enthusiastic. A small group of reviewers, writing mostly in large-exposure newspapers, was highly critical of *Blue Calhoun* in regard to two matters, the same two, incidentally, for which many other reviewers praised the novel: Price's depiction and treatment of his women characters, and the voice and credibility of his narrator.[17] Both of these points bear discussing and will be addressed in the pages ahead.

ARTISTS AND OUTLAWS

Though the personal letter is a much-praised hallmark of Price's fiction and takes up sizable portions of many of his novels, *Blue Calhoun* is his first epistolary novel. Hardly typical of the epistolary form, which most often contains numerous letters written to and from a variety of characters and voices, *Blue Calhoun* is made up entirely of a single letter, 373 pages in length, that comes from the voice of one person. Michiko Kakutani refers to the novel as "surely one of the longest letters in literary history."[18] The risk for Price is whether he can pull this off: can he maintain the reader's interest over the course of such a long letter, and is it credible that Blue, or anyone, would actually write such a long letter?

The letter is written by Blue to his fifteen-year-old grand-daughter, Lyn Kirkpatrick, whom he refers to as "my darling." A recent orphan (her mother died of breast cancer, and her father committed suicide), Lyn was also a victim of sexual abuse at the hand of her late father, Dane Kirkpatrick. Presently, in June of 1986, Lyn is living just outside of Raleigh with Luna Absher Adams, Blue's former lover; Luna's son, Anson; and Blue—though Blue has just left for Germany to settle the estate of Lyn's recently deceased parents. Ostensibly, Blue is writing his letter for two reasons: explanation and mercy. Since Lyn blames him for the death of her father—Blue's accidental observation of an incestuous scene between Dane and Lyn triggered Dane's suicide—Blue feels a need to explain to her not only the circumstances which ultimately led to that death but also the "literal facts on the actual people that stand behind the cells of your mind."[19] In other words, Blue needs to explain to Lyn, as fully and as truthfully as he can, his own story and the story of Lyn's mother so that she can see the kind of problems her family has tended toward, the hope being that she can avoid making the same mistakes. Though Blue does not ultimately feel responsible for Dane's death, he blames himself for virtually every bad thing that happens in his life, and for these things he is asking his granddaughter's mercy and forgiveness.

What one realizes after finishing Blue's narrative is that he spends very little time discussing Lyn, her father, or the specific circumstances leading to the father's death. Instead the novel concentrates on an event nearly thirty years prior: Blue's consuming attraction to and relationship with a teen-aged girl, young enough to be his daughter, named Luna Absher. The adulterous relationship—which lasted approximately one year, from April of 1956 to Easter of 1957—generated one of the most intense periods in Blue's life and nearly destroyed his marriage and family. Surprisingly, Blue describes his affair with Luna with great candor and passionate detail, no doubt fueling one of the earlier-stated criticisms of the novel, namely its credibility: why would a man of sixty-five write such a candid and, as one reviewer says, "sordid" letter to his abused and vulnerable granddaughter—a letter documenting his adulterous passion for a teen-aged girl who at the time of the affair was only one year older than this granddaughter herself?

The answer is complex. First, one must remember that Blue is not necessarily writing this letter solely for his fifteen-year-old granddaughter. The letter is actually delivered not to Lyn but to Luna, who will determine whether such a letter is suitable for Lyn to read, at this or any age. As Blue says in his opening remarks, "I've had to write it for a person older than you are now, a good deal older—the person you'll be in time" (1). In addition, Luna can decide if the letter is suitable only by first reading it herself; thus she will be the initial reader of Blue's letter. One must then question how much the letter is actually written for Luna, particularly since Blue has recently proposed to her (the final word of Blue's letter, perhaps echoing Joyce's *Ulysses,* is the very word he wishes to hear from Luna: "Yes"). One certainly wonders what role Blue's desire to wed Luna plays in his telling.

Another explanation for why Blue would write such a letter is Price's conviction that one's life is to some degree determined by one's heredity. In light of the behavior of Lyn's ancestors— Blue's drunkenness and adultery, Myra's and Mattie's stoicism and apparent need for suffering—Blue thinks it wise to tell Lyn the whole truth about her people. He also feels responsible for Lyn's problems to the extent that he believes in the domino effect: his affair with Luna tripped a series of events, including Mattie's marriage to and eventual rejection of Dane, which culminated in Dane's sexually abusing his daughter and then leaving her an orphan. Because of his guilt, in a genetic and behavioral sense, Blue believes he must tell Lyn everything, and since she has "already faced more than most generals," he senses she can handle it.

A final explanation for why Blue would write such a letter to his granddaughter, and one perhaps less generous to Blue, is that he has a history of offering too much too fast to teen-aged girls. His letter to Lyn mirrors his behavior with Luna thirty years prior; in each instance his intensity and his refusal to hold back drive him further, either sexually or verbally, than is socially accept-able. Though most people would not write such a letter to their granddaughter, most would also not in middle age have a sexual relationship with a sophomore in high school; however, Blue is not most people, and he does both.

One final point to keep in mind, particularly in regard to why Blue writes such a long and candid letter, is that he absolutely loves to talk and tell stories. A career salesman who explains that "Stories are something I'm better at than life" (3), Blue carries to his writing the same level of intoxication and intensity he carries to other aspects of his life. Blue has an addictive personality—he is addicted to alcohol, to flesh, to talk—and it is no surprise to find that this sexually charged man is also verbally charged. Unlike his verbally and sexually repressed wife, Myra, Blue is a talker, a voluble man who has no trouble getting the words out and freeing himself in the process.

Blue's rebirth or downfall—whichever way one decides to read it—begins on 28 April 1956 when Luna Absher and her mother, Rita, enter Atkinson Music Company, the store where Blue works, to buy an Autoharp. Luna appears siren-like, her voice not only rich and powerful but literally the part of her which Blue experiences first, before he even sees her. When Rita then tells Luna to sing, Blue, who is already aware of her power over him, says to himself, "*Don't, girl, please don't. I'm doing so good in this new life*" (10). What is most interesting about Blue's attraction to Luna, however, is not her voice or looks, though both are appealing, but the way Blue associates her with the other women in his life. For instance, when he first hears Luna sing, he is reminded of "how my mother's voice had sounded when I was a boy across her lap in the white porch swing on summer nights"; and when he arrives home from work that evening and sees his thirteen-year-old daughter, Mattie, he observes that Mattie's "deep blue eyes were straight from my mother" and that the eyes of both Mattie and his mother "all but equaled Luna's in darkness" (10, 13). Blue then describes Mattie, who is only three years younger than Luna, as "rushing to be a woman, too fast for me. . . . poised so near the edge of that peak," and moments later he wants "to rush Matt into the car and flee west with her that minute for good"—an action he will later attempt with Luna (13, 15). The point is that Blue's attraction to Luna has strong associations with his attraction to and love for both his daughter and mother.

The connection between Luna and Mattie is physically oriented: they are close in age, have similar eyes, and are described at one point by Blue as wearing similar attire —dark navy shorts and a blouse. Blue often draws parallels between them: "Luna could easily be my daughter" (83); "[Luna] seemed no bigger to hold than Mattie Calhoun" (247). In addition, Blue begins to pursue Luna just around the time when Mattie is readying for boys, which suggests two possibilities: Blue needs to love someone who resembles Mattie before she abandons him by falling in love with others boys; through Luna, Blue is able to realize vicariously a sexual relationship with his maturing daughter. Blue himself as much as admits a sexual attraction to Mattie: "When [a man] lives every day of his life in close home quarters with a budding girl, his soul gets tested instant by instant"; and after Mattie finishes singing to Blue, he writes, "I sat through those next minutes by Madelyn and fought my skin. My skin and the hungry pit of my mind that kept saying *Touch her. See how far you go*" (101). Again in Price's work, the love between parent and child proves particularly intense with incestuous overtones, yet Blue, unlike Dane, is able to resist the pull toward the actual act of incest.[20]

As much as Luna figures in Blue's relationship with his daughter (and vice versa) she also figures in his relationship with his mother. Blue, who works at a music store, associates both women with music: not only do Miss Ashlyn and Luna sing identical songs for Blue, but both had planned on lives in music. In addition, Blue states that with Luna he experiences the kind of love and physical kindness he has not known "since my mother would smile and watch me nurse her dry" (90). Blue's childhood bond with his mother was apparently the most intense and meaningful love in his life, yet by adolescence he realized that "my young mother would never be mine in any one of the thousand ways I longed to know her" (50); Miss Ashlyn would always be beautiful yet "past [Blue's] reach" (182). Through Luna, Blue is attempting to recapture that ideal relationship which he believes he once shared with his young and attractive mother.

Beyond the issue of how Blue's relationships with the various women in his life merge and interfuse, one needs to consider Price's depiction of the women themselves: Luna, Myra, Mattie, Rita, and Lyn. Reviewers voiced three basic complaints about the female characters in *Blue Calhoun:* they tend toward idealization ("they are endlessly sweet, loving and forgiving"); they are not strong or independent enough ("If any of the women in [Blue's] life had any strength or complexity at all, she'd tell Blue to get in his car and keep driving"); and they are forced to suffer excessively ("What are we supposed to make of all this female suffering?").[21] Though such criticism warrants attention, what complicates the issue is that an equal number of critics have praised *Blue Calhoun* explicitly *because of* Price's cast of strong, believable, interesting female characters: "[Price's] women are vivid, strong characters. . . . his most interesting characters"; "[Blue] is surrounded by a constellation of strong women"; "Price again demonstrates . . . how perceptively he writes of women."[22] As with *Kate Vaiden,* questions involving gender are particularly interesting and critically polarizing, and this area seems as good as any for future critical debate.

As for the three specific criticisms of Price's female characters—that they are idealized, weak, and severely punished—the one which rings truest is the first, yet that judgment is mitigated by the fact that Blue, as narrator, is the one with the tendency to idealize women, not Price. As for the second point, concerning the weakness of his females, Price himself answers his detractors by stating, "Some younger women reviewers have taken the line that any woman in her right mind would have told Blue Calhoun to pack his gear and leave. Wrong! Women in the '50s, in the sort of world Blue comes from, would never have told him to get out. Women put up with whatever the situation was. Men were continuously forgiven and welcomed back into the fold."[23] Thus one must understand the historical and cultural context to evaluate the relative strengths of Price's women. As for the third point, that Price's cast of females is unfairly punished with pain and early death, consider for comparison the fate dealt to the men in the novel: Bob Barefoot, leukemia and early death; Dane Kirkpatrick, suicide; Luther Bapp, the loss of a hand, and homelessness and illness; and Blue Calhoun, loss, pain, and suffering. In terms of gender, Price seems fairly equitable in his distribution of fate's cruelty.

To conclude, it is essential to address two significant questions with which the novel continuously plays. First, what force or impulse—fate, God, free will—is behind and responsible for the actions of Blue and the other characters? And second, how, morally speaking, does one feel about Blue? As for the first question, one cannot help but notice how often Blue invokes fate or its equivalent: "I have to leave you tonight, and it could be for good if fate says *Quit*" (1); "in my bad times I still suspected that all our lives were worked someway by iron invisible strings that we couldn't touch or change" (39); "Fate's the magnet that draws and wrings you" (118). Though Blue is not deterministic and largely accepts responsibility for his actions, he nevertheless suggests that the sky or God plays an additive role in human affairs. For instance, Blue believes the fervent prayers of those Catholic women surrounding him, Mattie and Myra, may play some role in deciding or moving fate, and he attributes to fate the nearly identical dreams concerning melting faces which he and Mattie experience: "*Fate's up to its old cat's cradle games*" (178). In addition, Blue suggests fate plays a role in the coincidences and strange meetings which occur in his life. For instance, even after he decides to separate from Luna, circumstances beyond free will bring them back together, as if their relationship were guided by "the hand of fate" (note that Price continually plays with the word *hand* in this novel, not only in regard to fate, but also as the word relates to touching, abusing, loving, signaling, communicating, writing, and revealing the future). Blue believes God possesses a balance ledger, distributing divine justice according to how one's "decencies" weigh against one's "debits" (312). This system of accounting applies not only to individuals but also to nations: Blue interprets the death of American soldiers in Vietnam as a payback for America's debt in having "exterminated all but the last American Indian" (296). As in much of Price's work, greater forces than the purely human are at work; as Blue states, "I still believe in some brand of justice bigger than our poor cops and courts" (347).

As for the second question—what does one think of Blue morally?—it is difficult not to like him, even though he abandons his wife and daughter to run off with his teen-aged lover. Much like Updike's Rabbit Angstrom, Blue is a man of natural impulse, desire, and hope who dreams of going South and escaping confinement and domesticity. Yet Blue is more genteel, articulate, and saintly than Rabbit. If goodness is defined by Blue's wife, Myra, who epitomizes sacrifice, selflessness, and the repression of natural instinct, then Blue is certainly not good. Yet his kindness and his desire to touch and save others make him far more likeable and human than Myra. In fact, one senses that it may be Myra's goodness which Blue is reacting against, and which leads him to sin and destructiveness. Though one may not wish to be married to Blue, he is a fascinating character, a rich voice, a man of tremendous energy and even saintliness.

Love and Work

More than twenty five years after its publication, *Love and Work* remains Price's most unusual work, a genuine departure from what one typically finds in a Reynolds Price novel. First, it is not rooted, as are Price's other nine novels, in the South;[24] instead the setting, the town of Fenton, is geographically nonspecific and could be virtually anywhere in America. Further, the natural world of trees, springs, woods, and broomstraw fields—the common fixture of Price's rural South—is virtually ignored.

Love and Work is, by contrast, Price's most indoor and internal novel, the one in which his characters are seen primarily in rooms and houses, and behind closed doors. As Price has pointed out, the narrative takes place on "a very small, narrow, almost classical French stage with bare properties, bare settings, and continually one or two characters speaking in very intense voices."[25]

Second, Price's two main characters are named rather plainly Tom and Jane—a departure from the inventory of rich and memorable southern names which he usually gives to his protagonists: Rosacoke Mustian, Wesley Beavers, Hutchins Mayfield, Bridge Boatner, Bluford Calhoun. Perhaps Price's decision not to bestow such rich regional names upon Tom and Jane relates to their being his least likable, most satirically drawn protagonists. Of Tom and Jane, Price has said, "they are such whey-faced, serious observers of their own minds that they have little time for the kind of verbal pageantry that comes as second nature to the Mustians . . . Mayfields and the Kendals."[26]

Third, *Love and Work* is far more cerebral, febrile, and psychologically tense than Price's other novels. Though he typically draws readers into the heads of his protagonists, there is in *Love and Work,* as Price has explained, "a kind of tension, a kind of tightened-forehead atmosphere" not often present in his other novels.[27] In *Love and Work* one undergoes with Tom Eborn every minor sensation and tremor—an experience which produces in one an edginess, discomfort, and occasional claustrophobia.

Finally, and in relation to its cerebral nature, *Love and Work* stands apart from Price's other novels in regard to style and tone.

ARTISTS AND OUTLAWS

The rich, ample, and lavish sentences of the Mustian novels, and the colloquial, metaphor-laden prose of later works like *Kate Vaiden* or *Blue Calhoun,* are nowhere to be found in *Love and Work.* Instead, Price utilizes, as he does in *Permanent Errors,* a spare, compressed, and tense prose style which tries to imitate the thought processes of Tom Eborn. While perhaps Price's most dense and poetic novel, *Love and Work* is also his darkest and most confining; likewise, while probably Price's least accessible and least entertaining novel, *Love and Work* may also be his most challenging and richly ambiguous.

All of this, though, is not to suggest that *Love and Work* has nothing in common with the rest of Price's work. Actually the novel deals with most of the same conflicts one typically finds in Price's writing: family or love vs. work, freedom vs. responsibility, isolation vs. community, love of spouse vs. love of parents. In addition, the novel explores what has become familiar territory in Price: an individual's curiosity about and obsession with the lives of his parents, the artist's relationship to his work, and the mysterious transmission of supernatural messages and information. In other words, if *Love and Work* is a departure in regard to character, setting, and style, it nevertheless deals with the same themes and obsessions that dominate in Price's oeuvre.

When it appeared in 1968 *Love and Work,* unlike Price's first two novels, received a mixed and less-than-enthusiastic reception. Negative criticism typically faulted the novel for being pretentious, contrived, overly stylized, and excessively cerebral, with a humorless, self-centered protagonist. Though positive reviews outnumbered the negative, most were qualified in their praise, viewing *Love and Work* as a necessary if not altogether successful step in Price's evolution as a writer. As Granville Hicks stated, "I am not so excited by this novel as I was by the other two, but I recognize it as a substantial achievement."[28] Only a handful of critics—Marston LaFrance, Louis D. Rubin, Jr., Francis King—voiced unqualified praise for Price's third novel and were able to penetrate to the core of its meaning. As the reviewer for the *Times Literary Supplement* accurately remarked, "This kind of writing ["the preciosity-cum-intensity of Mr. Price's style"] is not very fashionable now. Mr. Price's willingness to have a try at it seems therefore all the more exhilarating."[29]

Love and Work—at 143 pages, Price's most compact novel—is divided into four sections, each covering a period of less than twenty-four hours. In the first section Tom Eborn is at work on an essay upon the value and significance of work when he is interrupted by a ringing telephone. The caller is his mother, and though he does not take the call, he later tries to make reparations by driving thirty miles to see her. Once there, he learns from her friend, Ida Nolan, that she has since suffered a stroke; a short time later she dies. Eborn returns home and, rather surprisingly, recommences work on his essay.

The second section takes place several weeks later, after Eborn's mother has been buried. Eborn's wife, Jane, has read his essay on work and is angered and scared by the coldness of his words—that he could value family and friends so much less than his all-precious work. The next day Eborn cleans out his parents' home, attempting to sever all ties to the past. On the drive home he comes upon an automobile accident and finds a young man dying; frightened, he offers little assistance. That same evening over dinner with friends, Eborn is seized with "clenched terror" and excuses himself from the table.

ARTISTS AND OUTLAWS

The third section is dominated by the beginning of Eborn's novel-within-the-novel, his attempt to rescue his parents from what he imagines to be their obscure, futile lives. The novel, in which Eborn imagines his parents' first meeting at a skating pond, has given him a new sense of power, but this is jeopardized when Jane criticizes his work-in-progress. Their discussion is interrupted by news of a break-in at his parents' house.

The fourth section takes place on the same night and begins with Jane and Eborn's arrival at his parents' house. After an initial search, the police arrive. The only sign of entry is human excrement on the kitchen floor. Ida discloses Eborn's mother's final undelivered message—that on the evening before she died she saw her husband's ghost—and Ida maintains the ghosts have returned, are there with them now. The novel ends with his parents' ghosts, bathed in light, appearing before Eborn in the kitchen. Though he refused his mother's message in the opening scene, this message and appearance cannot be shut out. Entirely real to Eborn, the vision reveals that his parents need neither him nor his work to redeem their lives. Their love—a kind of love he himself is incapable of experiencing—sustains them. It is a memorable, astonishing final scene, and like nearly all moments involving the supernatural in Price, it is wonderfully ambiguous.

Though *Love and Work* is not difficult to summarize, it certainly is challenging to interpret. One reason is that the narrative focuses so intensely upon Eborn and his interior world that one is never able to move far enough away to see him clearly. Instead of being a flaw, though, this tightness and sense of containment within Eborn's consciousness is what gives the novel its personal and febrile intensity. Another factor making the novel difficult is that Eborn is not, at least on the surface, an everyman figure; rather, he is an emotionally cold and highly self-conscious intellectual whose thought processes are labored and complex. Finally, the novel is difficult because it offers mysteries and ambiguities which Price does not neatly tie up. For instance, one is never quite certain how Eborn's dreams reflect upon his life; how his personal life, or love, interacts with his writing, or work; or how the automobile accident relates to other events in the novel.

The greatest mystery, though, is Price's attitude toward Eborn. Initially one is inclined to believe Price has little sympathy for his protagonist and is largely poking fun at the highly self-conscious and cerebral writer, yet consider just how much of Price there actually is in Eborn. Eborn's essay on work comes almost word for word from a previously published Price essay entitled "Finding Work"; the photograph of Eborn's parents which serves as a "guide" for his novel-within-the-novel is identical to the photograph of Price's own parents from the cover of *Permanent Errors;* and Eborn's description of that photograph again is virtually verbatim from an earlier Price sketch entitled "My Parents, Winter 1926," also from *Permanent Errors.*[30] Finally, Price admits how "a great deal" of his own mother is in the character of Lou, and Price's brother, Bill, adds, "[The] novel-within-the-novel is about a couple based on our parents during the 1920s. . . . [Reynolds] imagines what they were like then and makes me believe it."[31] For the knowledgeable Price reader, a Philip Roth-like scenario emerges in which autobiography and fiction merge and become indistinguishable.

Is Price then Eborn, and is he poking fun of the self-conscious, overly analytical artist in himself who resists, is perhaps incapable of, emotional commitment? Perhaps. Yet as

Price explains in an interview, "I'm a nicer person than Thomas Eborn, at least more approachable. He's a very dried and balked man."[32] Though Price endorses much of what Eborn thinks and says, particularly about work, he simultaneously exposes the blindness and narcissism of Eborn's thinking. Eborn is no doubt the coldest, most distant of Price's protagonists—a far cry from such likable talkers as Rosacoke Mustian and Blue Calhoun—and one is never quite sure of Price's attitude toward him. Yet there is also something unusually human about the psychologically intense Eborn, who is a kind of blunted but exposed nerve. Though he may confuse or disappoint some readers, Eborn seems to reflect the author's attempt to reveal in raw fashion that side of himself which is most self-absorbed and unappealing.

Much as the opening sentence of *A Long and Happy Life* offers a miniature of the entire novel, presenting an image which captures the novel's central conflict, the opening scene of *Love and Work* operates in a similar fashion. Price begins with an illuminating image of Tom Eborn in his study with the door closed, trying to work while the telephone is ringing in the other room:

> He stood between desk and door, hands clenched, jaws grating, while each ring screwed deeper. . . . Urgent business. Refuse all calls. But calls were calls for help. That had been his belief since twelve years before—the call in the night, the rush to his father, the sight of that death.[33]

The novel's primary conflicts—love vs. work, freedom vs. responsibility—are revealed in this scene. Eborn is confronted with the dilemma of remaining behind the door, isolated and working, or answering the call, exiting the internal world of his mind for the external world of other people and their messages. The image of the introspective Eborn, caught and unable to move comfortably between the worlds of isolated work and community, is central to the novel. Price offers a portrait of the artist as a small, selfish, private man who goes to great lengths to shield and protect himself. In a novel which relies heavily on the imagery of doors, doorways, rooms, and houses, Eborn is the man trapped in the empty room of his own mind. Walling out chaos, love, and dependency is Eborn's strategy; all that matters is the quiet, solitary priesthood of work.

A weakness perhaps of *Love and Work* is that Eborn is so extreme in his reverence for work that many readers may have trouble either identifying with him or appreciating Price's satire of his character. Whether it be for writing or teaching, Eborn channels all of his energy into the creation of what he sees as useful work. In tandem with this belief, he feels his parents largely wasted their lives by not finding useful creative work and by deluding themselves into believing in the "fatal error of Western Man!—'that you are mine and I am yours'" (27). Such trusting, all-consuming love is simply a lie to Eborn, a man largely incapable of love, and he fervently believes his parents led lives of boredom, self-deception, and futility.

It is Eborn's wife, Jane—the Janus figure, the guarder of gates and doorways, in the novel—who reveals to Eborn how his attitude toward work is walling out love in his life, particularly hers. Yet Eborn is hardly ready to curtail or moderate his work; instead he comes upon an interesting, though again self-deceptive, strategy which demands even more work. Eborn decides that through work he can "repair his parents' [lives] . . . discover in their lives the available truth they had died without—and endure without (the lives of his parents being now at his mercy)" (79). Thus Eborn believes that through his novel-within-the-novel, in which he will fuse love and work, he can redeem his parents' way of life and also his own: the novel will be "a work of love which will find exactly that—that love can be work" (107). Yet Jane tells him his project is "easy lies," something he appears to understand at the end when he experiences the vision of his parents' ghosts. He sees that his parents do not need him and realizes they do not need saving. Their love was more powerful and redeeming than anything in his life, particularly his work. And so an epiphany lies at the end of the novel as Eborn sees the extent of his self-deception. Or does he? As with so many Price endings, one is not quite sure.

Though they are dead for most of the novel and together make only a brief ghostly appearance at the end, Eborn's parents play a significant role and exert, through their absence, the primary pressure in Eborn's mind. Nearly all of the major action in the novel—the death of his mother, Lou; the closing of the family home; Eborn's effort to immortalize and rescue his parents through his work; the break-in at his parents' home—relates in some way to Eborn's parents. As Price remarks, "The final vanishing of the parental generation is a very rocky passage. It certainly was for me, and *Love and Work* was the most immediate visible response to that passage."[34] Price, who suffered what he calls "a bona fide old-fashioned breakdown" not long after his mother's death, says in his memoir *Clear Pictures,* "Whatever steps a grown human being takes toward building his or her own hearth, in a central part of his mind, he's a child till his parents are dead. Only then, with no backer behind him or shield in front, must he really face the reality of death—*You are next in line.*"[35] Thus the significance of Eborn's name becomes apparent: as the prefix "e" suggests, he is "not" born or has not yet been born. With his parents suddenly gone, however, he is forced, at the age of thirty-four, to emerge into a new existence. As Eborn states after clearing through and then burning his parents' possessions: "Now I breathe new air. My life begins" (70). Yet by the novel's end, Eborn's life seems hollow and holds little promise, particularly in contrast to the lives of his parents.

Like so much of Price's fiction, *Love and Work* is concerned with the continuity of family, from parents to children, generation to generation, yet with the sudden emergence of Tom and Jane Eborn as the eldest survivors in their family, the future, not unlike their marriage, appears doomed. Though marriages typically fail in Price's work, husbands and wives play a crucial social role—a fact reflected in Price's epigraph from act 1 of Hofmannsthal's libretto to Strauss's *Die Frau ohne Schatten:*

You husbands and wives, who lie in one another's loving arms,
you are the bridge across the gulf
over which the dead come back to life!
Hallowed be your work of love![36]

The lines, sung by the nightwatchmen in the opera, are in praise of marriage and parenthood, though they are ironic when applied to both the opera and Price's novel. Price's Tom and Jane, like Barak and his wife from the opera, are hardly lying in "one another's loving arms"; if anything, their lovemaking is deceptive and less than loving. In addition, one finds in the opera that the female protagonist, the Empress, is miserable because she cannot cast a shadow (become pregnant), which will soon cause her husband, who is guilty of self-seeking love, to turn to stone. A parallel situation resides in *Love and Work*. Tom and Jane are childless after seven years of marriage—could a child perhaps save this marriage?—and Tom, selfishly feeding himself through his work, has essentially turned to stone.

In the opera, though, there is redemption and hope. The Empress learns the power of self-sacrifice, saving herself, her petrified husband, and Barak and his wife; and she acquires the ability to cast a shadow. Thus she looks forward to a future of children and domestic bliss. In contrast, *Love and Work* ends on a less optimistic, more ambiguous note. Eborn seems incapable of the Empress's self-sacrifice and love, and though the "the dead come back to life" in the novel's astonishing conclusion, Tom and Jane stand as a pathetic and failed "bridge" whose "work of love" will never be "hallowed."

The Tongues of Angels

The genesis of *The Tongues of Angels* is unique in that it was, according to Price, "pried from me by hypnosis."[37] During the summer of 1987, Price underwent biofeedback training and hypnosis to deal with the horrific pain that came from spinal surgery and resulting paralysis. Designed "to distance [his] pain without conscious urging," the hypnosis proved successful and provided an additional bonus: Price began to recall detailed and seemingly forgotten early memories, "reclaim lost stretches of my childhood and youth."[38] Many of those memories went into the creation of a memoir, *Clear Pictures* (1989), and still others, centering upon the ten weeks in the summer of 1953 which Price spent as a counselor at a boys' camp in the Blue Ridge Mountains, led to *The Tongues of Angels* (1990). Remarkably, Price wrote the first draft of *Tongues* in two weeks; as he states, "No previous books had tumbled from me at such a high clip of speed and pleasure."[39]

Though speed of composition presumably has little bearing on the quality of a work, in Price's case it led to one of his better novels and certainly his finest exploration of the role of the artist. *Tongues* may lack the scope of *The Surface of Earth* and the familial intensity of *The Source of Light,* yet it is Price's most visual and clearly imagined novel—one in which setting, character, and scene generate a memorable pictorial presence.[40] Because Price generally provides very little detailed physical description of his characters—he believes it a futile task and is more interested in generating a character's "emotional presence"[41]—his stories and novels are more often "felt" than "seen." One could also say, because of the rich voices of his narrators and speakers, that Price's work is more often "heard" than "seen." *Tongues,* though, offers a clear visual sense both of characters— Chief Jenkins, Rafe Noren, Bright Day, Kevin Hawser—and landscape: the Smoky Mountains, the layout of Camp Juniper, the prayer circle.

One explanation for the clarity and intensity of the novel's vision is that in regard to setting, Price was writing, more than in any of his other novels, from memory:

Once I tapped on my memory, it rolled open a long file-drawer whose existence I thought I'd forgot—the weather,

ARTISTS AND OUTLAWS

the plants and beasts of a place and time, the local songs and jokes, the dining customs (even the way we raffled extra desserts). . . .[42]

In addition the work's unique visual sense arises from the fact that this is the first Price novel to be narrated by a painter. Though Price's other artist-protagonists such as Hutch Mayfield, Thomas Eborn, and Charles Tamplin are watchful, none is quite so visually attuned to the world as Bridge Boatner.

As reviewers noted, one of the great accomplishments of *The Tongues of Angels* is Price's ability to capture, visually and emotionally, the experience of camp life and of being a youth in the early to mid-1950s. Yet in spite of its attention to various camp customs and activities, *Tongues* is hardly just a nostalgic evocation of the past. Rather it is a visionary novel, a work of spiritual dimensions which demonstrates specifically how mysticism operates in the relationship between an artist and his subject (remember that Price's understanding of "mysticism" suggests a "religious experience . . . directly between a given creature and what he perceives to be the Creator").[43] The beauty of *The Tongues of Angels* is that Price posits a world in which the Creator can be glimpsed, and thus partially known, beneath the surface of the natural world, an idea which appeared in less developed form in *The Surface of Earth*. For the watchful and spiritually attuned, such as Bridge Boatner, the possibility of knowledge and love comes from a committed and careful exploration of mountain horizons, human faces, and tragic events.

Tongues is a novel about seeing and learning how to see. Though seeing clearly is particularly important to Bridge because he is a landscape painter, Price suggests it is edifying and beneficial for all, and he demonstrates through Bridge and his campers how one's coming of age involves, among other things, seeing more clearly. The world, whether it be a landscape or a face, is not what it first appears to be—the lines are more complicated than one realizes—and so one must begin to look more carefully, to see beneath the surface and discover the secrets of the world and its Creator. As Bridge states, "*Look, really look. . . . Things don't often look the way you think they do. Pay them the simple honor of watching their lines and shadows till they tell you their secrets.*"[44] The watchful life, Bridge suggests, is ultimately rewarded; by watching, one becomes more devoted, respectful, and loving.

The ultimate observer, outside of the Creator, is the artist, particularly the visual artist who records the secrets of the world. As Bridge explains the painting he made that summer at camp, "What led me to the long horizontal west range" of the Smoky Mountains was that it contained "some coded combination of meanings that, if ever deciphered, would free mankind and forever reward us" (40). Though Bridge is exuberant and youthfully naive in his hopes, even titling his painting *The Smoky Mountains as the Meaning of Things,* he appears to be speaking for Price when he declares: "I was as sure then as now that most of the urgent outstanding secrets of this one universe are strewn here before us. They are barely encoded, in faces and things, and are patiently waiting for the witness that will solve them" (40). As an artist Bridge serves as the agent who attempts to see beneath the natural world to some divine center and who then offers a vision of what he has seen to others; in effect, he "bridges" the human and the divine, the physical and the spiritual.

ARTISTS AND OUTLAWS

In a novel more than peripherally interested in angels, the artist assumes an angelic role by delivering messages to humans from that divine core (recall that the word *angel* means "messenger" in Greek). Bridge, who like Price has been "fascinated by the fairly worldwide idea of angels," keeps an angel sketchbook in which he occasionally tries to "guess at the face of an angelic messenger" (87). Though Rafe Noren, who has the appearance of "a credible Angel Gabriel," is the primary angelic figure in the novel, Bridge aspires to and serves in a role angelic in nature. As an artist he is a middle- man between God and the world, and through his work he provides messages designed to inspire, edify, and actually "change men's souls" (51). Though Bridge is careful to deflate the ego of the artist when it grows too large, he nevertheless sees the artist in a grand role, providing the world with his gift of vision.

The Tongues of Angels is difficult to categorize because it is so many things: an initiation novel, a portrait of the artist, a love story, an elegy, and a mystical or visionary novel. As for how the novel fits within Price's oeuvre, *Tongues* closely resembles *Kate Vaiden* and *Blue Calhoun* in terms of narration and structure. Like those two novels, *Tongues* is a first-person narrative in which the speaker, an outsider or moral outlaw (Bridge is an artist), reflects upon a brief span of time in the distant past (thirty-four years earlier in his case), and attempts to reassess the actions and decisions of his younger self. Like Kate and Blue, Bridge is writing his story for a specific younger reader in his family: his son Rustum, who is planning a senior thesis on his father's early work. In addition, Bridge resembles Kate and Blue in feeling a strong sense of responsibility and guilt for his past; he writes early on that he may have caused Rafe's death, and the composition of his story is designed, at least in part, to come to terms with that death. Finally in *Tongues,* as in much of his fiction, Price returns to a historical period, the 1950s, and an age, the advent of adulthood, which prove particularly fertile for his creative sensibility, and he demonstrates how the distant and almost forgotten past continues to play a sizeable role in the present.

Though *Tongues* begins like other Price novels—a young protagonist on the verge of manhood is attempting to deal with the recent death of his father and stake out ground for himself as an artist (sounds like *The Source of Light*)—it differs from other Price novels in devoting relatively little attention to the protagonist's family. Bridge's father may be the impetus behind his son's ambition, and his father's recent death certainly weighs heavily on Bridge during his time at camp, yet the father, like Bridge's mother, is hardly developed as a character. Both parents, in fact, are largely forgotten by the end of the novel. As in *Love and Work,* the parents are more significant through their absence; because they no longer figure in Bridge's daily life, he must forge his own identity both as an adult and artist. *Tongues* then is the story of a different kind of family, a surrogate family. The protagonist, an only child, suddenly finds himself surrounded by brothers, sons, and fathers in a fraternal band of all-male campers (this is Price's first novel without a memorable female character). "Chief" Albert Jenkins, founder and owner of Camp Juniper, functions as the camp's fatherly presence, inspiring campers and counselors to rise to their physical and spiritual potential. Jenkins is assisted in his efforts by a large cast of wise and responsible men, a number of whom serve on occasion as guides for Bridge: Bright Day, a full-blooded Sioux and respected Indian teacher; Mike Dorfman, a skilled musician and anthropologist; Kevin Hawser, a gifted and brilliant fellow counselor. From Bridge's perspective, Jenkins places tremendous responsibility upon the counselors, and it is largely through Jenkins's trust that Bridge and the others mature and emerge as men.

The most crucial bond, though, which Bridge develops at camp is with Rafe Noren, a fourteen-year-old with extraordinary features and abilities. Physically, verbally, and spiritually advanced for his age, Rafe, like Wesley Beavers, is someone people like to watch; as Bridge says, he "showed stretches of majesty." A mutual attraction with erotic undertones develops between Bridge and Rafe, and the draw between them seems more powerfully charged than, say, Bridge's bond with his girlfriend, Viemme. Keep in mind though that Rafe's death, along with the passing of nearly thirty-five years, has colored, even distorted, Bridge's memory of their relationship; as Bridge says, "[Rafe's] eventual end was what made him grow so large in my mind" (164).

To a degree Bridge assumes a fatherly role with the younger Rafe: he teaches Rafe to see and draw, rescues and nurses him after his snakebite wound, and is even mistaken by a nurse for being Rafe's father. In addition, Bridge is able to come to terms with his father's death through Rafe, writing that he feels "satisfaction in being able to do for [Rafe] what I'd failed to do for my father" (141)—namely save him, though ultimately no one is able to save Rafe from his ruptured aneurysm. By tending to Rafe and his other campers, Bridge begins to assume the role his father left vacant.

Perhaps the two most useful facts to know about Rafe are that he has a tragic past, having witnessed the rape and murder of his mother, and that he has extraordinary ability as a dancer. One wonders, particularly since this novel is centrally concerned with the creation of art, whether Rafe's suffering and pain have led in some way to his precocious artistic abilities. Though Rafe does not, like Bridge, appear particularly ambitious or self-conscious about his abilities, he is nevertheless an artist, a gifted dancer who inspires and edifies others through his performances. He is also an angelic figure, not only by virtue of his name—the archangel Raphael is the guardian of youth and a "topnotch healer"—but through other physical characteristics: he wears wings, possesses "otherworldly looks," "throws a strong light," and appears as "a creature dropped in from Arcturus" (95, 190, 116). Finally, Rafe is the Christ-figure in the novel, whose early death forces one to question what his suffering and pain have provided for others. Bridge even refers to Rafe's as a "sacrificial life," and one questions to whom or for what Rafe has been sacrificed.

In the beginning of the novel, Bridge believes he had some role in Rafe's death, referring to it as "a death I may have caused. ... by ignorance, by plain lack of notice" (1). Though he may have unintentionally led Rafe toward danger, he realizes by the end "it was childish selfishness to think till now that I harmed Rafe badly or caused his death" (192). Rafe and his death, however, have played a crucial role in Bridge's development; as Bridge writes, "Rafe Noren's life is present deep under the lines I've drawn and especially the shadows" (172). Bridge's work has been shaped by and is in turn infused with Rafe and the mystery of his death. Though Bridge is careful not to suggest that Rafe's death was redemptive in its having furthered his own artistic development ("if I should mouth anything so shameful, I hope somebody blots me out" [191]), it is nevertheless Bridge's art, both his painting and his writing, which memorializes Rafe.

What Bridge learned from Rafe and what makes Rafe worthy of attention is the force of his character: his beautiful, charged presence, his laughter and warmth, the literal light he shed:

> Recall his name and some kind of picture against the light—a boy becoming an actual eagle or the generous giver of fire and warmth or laughing his way through mortal trial, denying his fate a few more days. (192)

Behind all of this, though, is love. As Bridge says, "love worked Rafe." Chief Jenkins adds that love worked Rafe "To death. It absolutely killed him" (179). In the passage from 1 Corinthians (13:1–13) which gives the novel its title is Price's reminder to his reader about what St. Paul says concerning the importance of love—note that Bridge interprets the word *charity* as "love," suggesting the love of God poured out in Christ:

> Though I speak with the tongues of men and of angels, and have not charity, I am become *as* sounding brass, or a tinkling cymbal. And though I have *the gift of* prophecy, and understand all mysteries, . . . I am nothing. . . . And now abideth faith, hope, charity, these three; but the greatest of these *is* charity.

In its entirety the passage argues that the great gift from God is not "tongues" or "prophecy" but *love*. Through the life of Rafe

Noren, an angel serving God's design, one is able presumably to glimpse God's love. Thus Price's novel reveals not only that the divine exists in the natural world, but also that spiritual messages are being transmitted through individuals such as Rafe Noren and through the work of artists such as Bridge Boatner. Angelic tongues are speaking to those who know how to see and hear.

CHAPTER FIVE

Man of Letters

Though Reynolds Price is known primarily as a novelist, novels account for less than half of his oeuvre. As of 1995, Price has published, in addition to the ten novels, four volumes of plays (six plays in all), four collections of short stories, three volumes of essays and translations, three volumes of poetry, and two volumes of memoirs. A "man of letters" in the fullest sense of the term, Price is highly competent and often brilliant in each genre to which he turns, and unlike others who have tried their hand widely, Price has no weak link. As a short story writer he has been compared to Hemingway, Joyce, Chekhov, Faulkner, Fitzgerald, Poe, O'Connor, and Welty, and his stories have appeared in the annual editions of *The Best American Short Stories* and *The O. Henry Prize Stories.* Guy Davenport refers to Price's second collection of stories, *Permanent Errors* (1970), as "a pivotal book in our literary history," and Ron Carlson adds that *The Collected Stories* (1993) "will exist somewhere as a thread in the fabric of twentieth-century American literature."[1] The same can be said for Price's abilities as a memoirist. Stephen Spender refers to Price's *Clear Pictures* (1989) as "a masterpiece,"[2] and a second volume of memoirs detailing Price's bout with cancer, *A Whole New Life* (1994), has generated more public attention than perhaps any other single Price volume.

The same high appreciation, interest, and acclaim exist for Price's work in other areas—translation, drama, poetry, and essays and criticism. Price's *A Palpable God,* a collection of

UNDERSTANDING REYNOLDS PRICE

biblical translations which includes an essay on the origins of narrative, was a finalist in 1978 for the National Book Award for translation, and the text was praised by Anthony Burgess, Frank Kermode, and Frederick Buechner. Burgess stated that Price's introductory essay "from now on must be required reading in creative-writing courses," and Kermode remarked that "if one wants to see how curiously [the Gospel of Mark's] power derives from its bald rough Greek, Price's translation is probably the best there is."[3] With regard to yet another genre, Price's plays have appeared on numerous stages across America and on public television's *American Playhouse.* David Patrick Stearns calls Price "a major playwright" and refers to Price's dramatic trilogy *New Music,* first produced in its entirety by the Cleveland Play House, as "the most ambitious piece of theater by a U.S. writer in years."[4] Finally, with regard to poetry, John Hollander, Toni Morrison, George Garrett, Robert B. Shaw, Spender, and others have offered praise for Price's poems, and Price has received the Levinson, Blumenthal, and Tietjens Awards from *Poetry.*

The intention here is not to suggest Price has matched the achievements in drama of, say, Pinter or Stoppard or, in poetry, of Merrill or Kinnell, but instead to underscore the fact that Price has proven himself a gifted craftsman in virtually every form of literary endeavor. Like his contemporaries John Updike and Joyce Carol Oates, Price is an extraordinarily versatile writer who excels in all genres and subgenres, and is worthy of attention regardless of the form in which he finds himself working.

One of the benefits, of course, in being an established novelist working in other modes is that one is able to publish, and generate considerable appreciation for, works that may not have otherwise made it into print. Were it not for Price's stature as a novelist, Atheneum would most likely not have taken a chance and published his first play, *Early Dark,* or his biblical translations, *A Palpable God.* Yet the other side of this coin, the disadvantage for someone like Price, is that his work in other genres, no matter how skillfully executed, will always be treated secondarily—as is indeed the case in this study. Price's memoirs, short stories, and biblical translations are perhaps as original and significant as anything appearing in these genres in contemporary American literature, yet they have received little critical attention.

Regardless of whatever intrinsic value one places on Price's "other" work, that work is of interest because of the light it sheds on his novels. Certainly Price's biblical translations and essays assist in understanding influences and pressures which have acted on the evolving style and themes of his novels. In addition, Price's essays cover a wide range of topics—the South and southern writers, his childhood, his own writings, literary guides, biblical and religious studies, and gender issues—and thus provide background material and offer new points of entry for a discussion of his fiction. Finally, his memoirs and poetry generate an image of the writer behind the novels while revealing the autobiographical seeds which have inspired his fiction—one learns that Kate Vaiden emerged from Price's mother, Elizabeth, for instance, and Rob Mayfield from Price's father, Will.

Because Price has produced such a large body of writing, many works must go undiscussed in this volume. Though his short stories offer his strongest writing outside of his novels, the works which have attracted the most popular attention in recent years, and which are thus the focus of this chapter, are his two volumes of memoirs.

Clear Pictures

Though *Clear Pictures* lacks the dramatic unravelling and stylistic flair of Price's novels, it is a brilliant and memorable work—"a masterpiece of a rare kind," says Stephen Spender, "reminding me of Thoreau's *Walden*."[5] Spender's comparison seems appropriate, though Price's work is hardly derivative; the similarities to *Walden* are mostly general in nature. For instance, *Clear Pictures* resembles *Walden* in being a singular work, unlike virtually anything in its genre. As a result of Price's unique sensibility and precociousness (at six he had his first mystical experience), his extraordinary powers of observation and memory (his recall extends back to when he was four or five months old), and his outward focus (Price directs attention away from himself toward those "guides" who proved crucial to his growth), *Clear Pictures* emerges as a distinct autobiographical work. In addition, like *Walden, Clear Pictures* is inspirational. Much as Thoreau rouses one to live closer to nature, Price implicitly stimulates his reader to be more observant and to plunge more deeply into one's own vast pools of forgotten memory. Finally, *Clear Pictures* demonstrates as does *Walden* that through a close and direct examination of the natural world—by "reading" nature, so to speak—one can gain entrance to a spiritual world. Though Price is more Christian mystic than transcendentalist, and though his concern is far more with people than with trees and ponds, his work bears a resemblance to Thoreau's.

For readers eager to learn Price's secrets or the intimate facts of his personal life, *Clear Pictures,* like the majority of memoirs penned by contemporary American writers, will disappoint. Though he mentions suffering a mental breakdown in the mid-

1960s, Price chooses not to explore that darkness, nor does he choose to expose the private details of his life as an adult. His focus in *Clear Pictures* is largely on others and the crucial roles they played in his development as a child, adolescent, and aspiring artist; the book in fact ends with Price's emergence as an adult, and thus his separation from family and community.

Though it is difficult to place *Clear Pictures* within any autobiographical tradition because of its singular nature, it fits more naturally within a southern rather than an American tradition—with Welty's *One Writer's Beginnings* bearing the closest resemblance. As Robert Atwan points out, "the southern autobiographical tradition has opposed Franklin's paradigm of the self-made man" because the southern writer "cannot easily imagine a life separable from family, kin, and region." In southern autobiographies Atwan finds "less stress upon the individual—no one is truly 'self-made'—and a greater emphasis on the individual's sense of belonging to a place, its people, and its way of life."[6] The core of Price's book concerns the ways these rather ordinary people—mostly white middle-class citizens of small North Carolina towns in the 1930s, 1940s, and 1950s—altered Price's life, encouraging and enabling him to develop into an artist and an adult. Much as Thoreau offers a tribute to nature, demonstrating how it influenced and inspired his life, Price offers his own tribute to what he calls "First Loves, First Guides": his parents, relatives, friends, and teachers.

What is perhaps most interesting about Price's memoir, historically speaking, is that it offers such a rich portrait of a time, place, people, and way of life that are now mostly gone—a pre-television world in which "you never thought of phoning your friends to ask if a visit was welcome; you just drove up."[7] In addition, the people to whom Price devotes such careful and extended attention are the type whom history and literature most often forget. The people of *Clear Pictures* are not powerful, wealthy, or brilliant, nor are their lives particularly adventurous or scandalous. They are ordinary people whose accomplishments and gifts are not known outside of their own homes or families, yet through their courtesy, patience, and love, they enable others, such as Reynolds Price, to attain important goals.

Price demonstrates that despite an obsession with solitude, the artist greatly needs other people for nourishment, love, and witness. In addition, Price reveals what he has long argued in regard to the question of literary influence: that the most significant influences are not, as Harold Bloom would contend, other writers and poets, but those individuals, mostly family and friends, whose voices, faces, and deeds have been dominant in the writer's life, particularly during his or her childhood and adolescence. As Price states in an earlier essay on literary influence, "The truest list of a novelist's influences . . . would be . . . a list not of other artists however grand but of private names. . . . My own list would begin: Elizabeth Price, Will Price, Will Price Junior, Ida Drake, Grant Terry."[8]

One of the achievements of *Clear Pictures* is Price's depiction of this cast of guides and influences: his parents, Will and Elizabeth Price; his relatives, Ida Rodwell Drake and Macon Thornton; black household servants, Grant Terry and Flora Rushing; teachers, Crichton Davis and Phyllis Peacock; and an assortment of other friends and artists. These individuals, as Price demonstrates, have taught him how to live, love, create, be alone,

MAN OF LETTERS

and finally die, and they have enabled him to develop his talents. Though some may argue that in preserving his childhood world Price depicts his characters as too decent and good-hearted, recall that in an almost continual refrain, Price confronts the primary evil of that world—racism: "How were so many otherwise intelligent, morally sensitive, watchful and generous people trapped in the running of a brute and tragic machine?" (77). Though Price does not gloss over or excuse the behavior of his family and relatives, he attributes their behavior to the very thing which handicaps and devastates so many of his own fictional characters, blindness and ignorance: "If you say that any two eyes should have seen the tragic cruelty of her kin and her race . . . , I'd make the elementary point that every American is sealed, at any moment of his or her life, in multiple forms of conscious or unconscious blindness" (79).

Certainly the most significant presence in Price's life was his father—who, Price writes, "meant more to me than anything else." A salesman, Will Price was also a brilliant comedian and mimic, a quick-change deceiver, and a fear-ridden hypochondriac. As for why Price feels his strongest connection with his father, there is, in addition to whatever mysterious principles lie beneath basic attraction, the all-important fact that Will sacrificed his drinking in order that his son and wife survive the life-threatening ordeal of childbirth. In addition to his great sacrifice, Will stood as a model of courtesy, and he taught his son how to love, how to tell stories and draw elephants, and perhaps most importantly, how to die: "Needlessly fearful as he'd always been, he was wild to show me, not only the blood rites of duty but a last and larger thing—the secret I'd need when my own end came: the naked reckless hunger to go" (299). Even Will's early death, at the age of fifty-four, is interpreted by Price as a gift in that it enabled him to move more quickly into his own adulthood.

As for the other figures Price discusses, each guides him in some specialized way. Ida Rodwell Drake, Price's aunt, educates him in the value and management of solitude, and his cousin Macon Thornton, in addition to providing financial support, gives Price "a deep-cut picture to study and learn" of a bachelor, "a single figure . . . consuming life gladly and giving it back" (147). Grant Terry, "the most important black presence in [Price's] life," teaches him the possibility for friendship and love between blacks and whites, and Flora Rushing, a cook and housekeeper, teaches Price about adult love and serves as a guide to sexuality. Others inspire and seduce him in the arts. Crichton Davis, who invited Price to her home to paint bottles, serves as a master teacher and an artistic admirer, and from her Price learns that art need not be a private game or secret pleasure but can be a shared activity. And Phyllis Peacock, Price's high school English teacher, provides the lesson that poetry not only matters but can change lives. Though Price's homage to these guides has the potential of becoming a disguised tribute to himself, the book avoids that trap, allowing these men and women to emerge as individuals who are as memorable and alive as the best characters in his fiction— which seems only fair, considering that these people are the voices, faces, and literal inspiration behind Price's fictional characters.

What one notices early on in *Clear Pictures* is something that is also apparent in, say, the autobiography of Henry James:

that one is in the presence not of an ordinary human being but an individual whose sensibility is unusually keen and perceptive— a genius, if you will. Price, for instance, claims that his first memory, in which he is lying in the sun while Topsy the goat eats his diaper, extends back to when he was only four or five months old, and he even speculates as to whether he possesses uterine memory. Later, as Price passes through childhood and adolescence, one observes the continued precociousness of his sensibility: as a sixth-grader in a small North Carolina town he fills his room with busts of Haydn and Mozart and a portrait of Chopin; and at fifteen he writes a screenplay about the life of Saint Bernadette. Though some readers may be put off by or question the reliability of Price's claims, he is not boastful or arrogant; he is simply blessed with unique intellectual and spiritual gifts.

Price is also blessed with narrative gifts which imbue his life story with drama, intensity, and poignancy. For instance, let us again consider Price's account of his birth. What is unique about this story is Price's manner of telling—the way he infuses his story with the biblical: his father "seals" a bargain with God, and Price, like Isaac, becomes both gift and hostage. Though once again some may accuse Price of pretentiousness or even arrogance for describing his birth in such grand terms, one must keep in mind that he has continually striven to bring to his work, and life, the intensity and mystery of biblical narrative. For Price, biblical stories speak closely to the core of spiritual and narrative hunger, and by alluding to these stories in writing about his own life, he demonstrates through personal example that human existence is neither insignificant nor arbitrary, but instead a vital and meaningful part of a larger design.

UNDERSTANDING REYNOLDS PRICE

In spite of his dramatic birth and his artistic genius, Price simultaneously functions as an everyman figure. The childhood and adolescent self about which he writes is hardly wealthy or famous, lists no great conquests or victories, and accomplishes little of note. His is not a childhood of Mozartian genius and success. Rather, Price's gifts have to do with memory, vision, and narrative, and it is through our appreciation of such gifts that the relationship between author and reader is established. Though there may be a tremendous gulf between his own sensibility and that of the reader, Price inspires us to believe that much more exists, both in the visible world and in memory, for us all to see and know. A continual refrain in this volume, and in Price's oeuvre, is that human beings are blind and need to look more carefully at the world: "In daily life and all later work, I tried to see clearer, steadier, deeper. No human being sees much. Our eyes don't begin to exhaust the spectrum of light. . . . But I try to go on seeing more" (303–04). In his pointing to a general human failure, and his attempting to overcome that failure, Price resembles Benjamin Franklin in his *Autobiography,* though Franklin was far more explicit and prescriptive in directing his readers toward improving their lives. Price simply makes readers aware, through his own example, of the largely untapped human potential in the areas of observation and memory.

In his captions for the thirty-five photographs in *Clear Pictures,* Price demonstrates what careful observation can reveal. For instance, consider the photograph of Price's parents at the opening of chapter one. Judging by their dress, the light, and the ring that is barely perceptible on Elizabeth's hand—how many readers ever look so carefully at a family photo?—Price reasons the time to be the early winter of 1926. Price further remarks that as a child he was "puzzled by the apparent absence of my father's left leg and by his and mother's strangely merged shadow" (16) in this picture. In an age in which one is besieged daily by numerous printed and electronic visual images, Price stands as one who continues to look carefully and patiently at what is before him. Another photo, of Price's father, Will, taken in 1918, demonstrates the care which Price uses in studying a face: "[Will] thinks he will soon be shipped away to the trenches of France and cannot know that the armistice of November 11th will save him. Unclouded yet by drink or care, his gray eyes burn with the hopeful fervor he'll fight to reclaim, fifteen years from now" (22). Price's observation of his father's face extends beyond the visible and present; he attempts to see that face in light of what the future will bring. Though Price does not direct readers to sift through old boxes of family photographs or undergo hypnosis to recover lost childhood memories, his example demonstrates what can be found and seen when one strives to look carefully.

A Whole New Life

Considering that *A Whole New Life* deals centrally with cancer, pain, and physical devastation, and is set in hospitals and rehabilitation clinics, one would entertain few hopes for the book's popular success. One might suspect that such a volume, like Price's collection of biblical translations, *A Palpable God,* would appeal to a limited, though well-seasoned and stalwart, audience. The surprise then is not only that *A Whole New Life* has been so successful commercially but that it has attracted more media attention than any other Price volume. Currently in its fifth printing, *A Whole New Life* has generated a three-page spread in *Time,* front-page reviews in the book sections of the *Washington Post* and the *Los Angeles Times,* and invitations from America's major news and talk shows. How has a book about devastating pain and illness attracted so much popular attention?

There are several good answers. First, cancer, which has wormed its way into millions of American families and homes, is along with AIDS the terror of the contemporary age. Any volume which serves, at least on one level, as a how-to book on battling the disease and overcoming the pain provides an important benefit to the afflicted and their families and friends. Second, because, as Price states, the "row of sane printed matter which comes from the far side of catastrophe" is so "very slim,"[9] an attempt by one with Price's literary abilities and perception is a welcome and much-needed commodity. As William Henry III writes, "Rarely if ever has a patient of Price's writerly gifts taken on the story of physical devastation."[10] Finally, and perhaps most crucially, Price survives. *A Whole New Life* is about a victory, miraculous in nature, and it leads to Price's final declaration that although he is now paralyzed and confined to a wheelchair, his present life is somehow better. Price is a survivor, and his story of overcoming limitations and transforming his life into something better is the kind that Americans particularly crave.

In many respects *A Whole New Life* could be placed in a tradition leading back to Emerson, Thoreau, and Whitman. Like those nineteenth-century writers, Price is optimistic about the self and its ability to see and know the world. In addition, Price believes the self possesses tremendous potential—which in his case was used to fight disease, overcome pain, and achieve a personal transformation. As the book's title suggests, his is "a whole new life." Further, just as those earlier writers were distrustful of and resistant to the orthodoxy and conformity of society, Price continually questions social institutions—for instance, the world of medicine and doctors—and resists commonly accepted social prescriptions, such as the notion that he should be angry and should then cathartically release the anger that he is feeling. Though Price is not, like Emerson, a transcendentalist, *A Whole New Life* follows the tradition of celebrating the self and its potential for growth and transformation.

A Whole New Life also has affinities with Price's first volume of memoirs, *Clear Pictures*—a fact suggesting the patterns in Price's personal writings. Though the subjects could not be more different—*A Whole New Life* is concerned with an illness and a healing, *Clear Pictures* with a child and artist's growth and initiation—there are similarities. First, though the volumes ultimately focus on Price himself, each simultaneously demonstrates that others have played major roles in his life and, in effect, that his survival and success have depended upon the assistance, love, and generosity of these other individuals. Second, each is inspirational in nature: *Clear Pictures* prompts readers to *look* at the world more closely and to plunge more deeply into pools of forgotten memory; *A Whole New Life* leads readers to a new awareness of one's individual potential for managing and overcoming pain and illness. Third, each demonstrates the therapeutic utility of art (writing, drawing, music), whether it be to fight off a cancerous tumor or the effects of a betrayal by one's peers. Art serves as a vehicle for generating energy and movement: in *Clear Pictures* Price uses writing to escape Warren County, and in *A Whole New Life* his drawing and writing aid him in warding off death. Finally, each volume—despite its general similarity to the other—is a highly original work. Price explains the impetus for *A Whole New Life:* "I needed to read some story that paralleled, at whatever distance, my unfolding bafflement—some honest report from a similar war, with a final list of hard facts learned and offered unvarnished—but again I never found it. . . . nobody known to me in America, or on the shady backside of Pluto, is presently offering useful instruction in how to absorb the staggering but not-quite-lethal blow of a fist that ends your former life and offers you nothing by way of a new life that you can begin to think of wanting" (181).[11] Thus, Price was drawn to write the very book he wanted to read but was unable to find.

Price's story begins in the spring of 1984, in what had "so far . . . been the best year of my life," when a colleague asked him during a walk why he was slapping his foot on the pavement. After a series of excruciating tests and radical spinal surgery, Price learned he was host to a malignant tumor, ten inches in length and "braided" in his spinal cord. Due to its sensitive location, the tumor could not be removed, and Price was forced to endure five weeks of high doses of radiation. Though Price was not told this at the time, a physician cousin informed Price's brother that Reynolds had "six months to paraplegia, six months to quadriplegia, six months to death" (32).

Price's physical deterioration was then fairly rapid. His legs continued to fail, he suffered burns on his neck and upper back from the radiation, and in a single night he experienced the collapse of his "gut": "My waist was suddenly ten inches bigger than it'd been the previous night" (78). In addition, his feet began to swell, the numbness in his legs and stomach climbed higher in his body, his face swelled and became a "sodden moon-face" from high doses of steroid, and eventually he lost use of his legs. By the summer of 1985, a year after his initial surgery, Price was confined to a wheelchair and suffering from incredible, debilitating pain.

The pain, which was his "constant companion" after the first surgery, became ferocious and intense: "There were times each day, for hours at a stretch, when my whole body felt caught in the threads of a giant hot screw and bolted inward to the point of screaming. At such times I'd lie on the bed, chew the corner of a dry pillowcase in dumb confusion . . ." (88). The doctors' solution was to prescribe an assortment of drugs (methadone, amitriptyline, tryptophan, and baclofen), which not only provided little relief from the pain but led to "a narcotized life." Price remained in such a state for two more years, though miraculously he produced several books during this period. Not until the summer of 1987 did he discover how biofeedback and hypnosis can be utilized in dealing with and overcoming the pain. In the meantime, medical breakthroughs—the MRI and the ultrasonic laser scalpel—offered a new chance for removal of the tumor. And in the fall of 1986, after two more radical surgeries (and another surgery to repair a leaking wound), Price was at last free of the eel. Though it would take another year to free himself from the pain, and two more years to wean himself from the drugs, he had essentially survived his battle with cancer, and as he states at the conclusion, his annual scans continue to show his spine clear of cancer.

In spite of its bleak subject matter, Price's story, as stated earlier, is appealing and accessible—what some might call a "page turner." No other Price volume, in fact, encourages such a rapid reading. One of the reasons is Price's style. *A Whole New Life* does not contain the stylistic complexities and demanding rhetorical patterns that Price's fiction does. For instance, one does not find the elaborate, protracted sentences of *A Long and Happy Life;* the compressed, tense, even "hieroglyphic" prose of *Love and Work;* or the lush, colloquial, metaphor-laden prose of *Kate Vaiden* or *Blue Calhoun.* Once again, Price generates a different style and voice. As physician and novelist Richard Selzer observes, Price "tells his story in a prose that is stripped down and pell-mell, utterly devoid of the pomp of language or the writer's vanity."[12] The style of *A Whole New Life* is perfectly suited to its subject—a subject whose seriousness and significance would have been undermined by such rhetorical flourishes as, say, Price's opening in *A Long and Happy Life.*

Another explanation for the book's appeal is that it confronts what is ultimately the most crucial issue for humans: mortality. Though the book is addressed "first to others in physical or psychic trials of their own, to their families and other helpers" (vii), Price is ultimately writing to everyone, since at some point everyone must confront devastation and dying. What is most attractive about Price's narrative, though, is how he casts the battle as one-on-one combat in which he, "the hero of an epic struggle," is driven to become as "resourceful as any hunted man in the bone-dry desert, licking dew from cactus thorns" (31). Referring to himself as Jonah and Job and inspired by a vision of Christ, Price gives his narrative biblical dimensions. The David and Goliath element is clearly present, with Price as the lone, weaker man forced to wage battle against a colossal giant—all-powerful Death—embodied in the eel which has gained control of his spinal cord.

Though there currently exists a stockpile of books from American publishers offering stories of individuals overcoming adversity, Price's is unique because, as has been said, it comes from one with rare literary abilities. Consider, for instance, Price's description of the "band of cripples" at the Duke rehabilitation clinic: "a swarming Hieronymus Bosch assortment of ludicrous damned souls in high torment" (107). And of the competent but emotionally cold and unavailing doctor, Price writes, "Maybe we have the right to demand that such a flawed practitioner display a warning on the office door or the starched lab coat, like those on other dangerous bets—*Expert technician. Expect no more. The quality of your life and death are your concern*" (146). Price is also aware of, and able to describe, sensations in his body which others, in writing about disease, seem to have missed or been unable to articulate: "The strange new sense of being suspended outside my body was also growing more frequent and lending my days an eerie unreality. . . . I'd rise from a chair and still feel seated for a curious moment till my mind caught up with the vertical action" (38). In addition, Price's experience as a seasoned writer leads him to resist the sentimentality and self-pity likely to befall such a narrative. He refers to himself as a "gimp," resisting such euphemisms as "disadvantaged, specially challenged or beatified-by-pain" (98), and though he is fortified by Christian faith, his attitude toward religion is not smug, easy, or alienating.

UNDERSTANDING REYNOLDS PRICE

Yet the most unique and surprising aspect of Price's narrative is his final claim: that his new life—as a man confined to a wheelchair and crucially dependent upon an assistant and burdensome medical supplies (catheters, extremity pumps)—is *better.* How could that be? Price offers two reasons. First, he has become more patient, watchful, and willing to listen—a condition that has made his "pool of human evidence" grow. And second, sexual desire has migrated from the center of his life to the edge—a fact that has contributed to the increased speed and volume of his work. Whether or not one fully accepts Price's claim, he reminds readers of how illness and adversity often create new strengths. For instance, though he has lost the use of his legs, Price has found compensation in other areas of his body: "I'll risk the claim that, from the time I left rehab, I've taken more pleasure than most adults ever come to know from my present eyesight, hearing and taste, from the stretches of my skin that still have feeling, and from my mind's new grip on patience" (102).

Though Price never claims that his book, in demonstrating the redemptive powers of adversity, is an attempt, like Milton's *Paradise Lost,* to explain or "justify the ways of God to men," the book does do just that. Milton scholar and biblical translator, Price questions whether a design is at work in the universe: "Given my morning at Lake Kinnereth, my recent liberation from pain, and the ongoing steady stream of work, was I meant to see an external pattern in my new life . . . ?" Though he is cautious about "reduc[ing] that weight of mystery to a trail of tea-leaves spelling a readable usable message" (176), Price is more than open to the possibility that an unseen creator is working the fate that has befallen him. Strangely, Price has fulfilled the prophecy of the title of his first book, which incidentally included a character paralyzed and confined to a wheelchair: he has lived and is living "a long and happy life." Like the prototypical American Adam, Price transforms himself into a new man; however, in his case transformation does not lead to tragedy and decline as it does for so many fictional characters in American literature. Instead he turns his own transformation into something positive and suggests that a mysterious, unseen hand is directing the action, leading him on through adversity toward a greater and fuller understanding of the world.

Conclusion

At the close of her valuable and thoughtful study of Price, Constance Rooke wrote in 1983, "The question of Price's stature relative to that of other twentieth-century American writers cannot yet be answered; too much depends upon the new directions that his work may take."[13] Though twelve years later it remains difficult to judge Price's stature or indeed that of any living writer, one now has the advantage of seeing those "new directions" his work has taken.

Central to any consideration of Price's evolution since 1983 is the fact that during the past twelve years he has published ten volumes of work that are not novels. Though he continues to be best known as a novelist, Price has emerged in recent years as one of contemporary America's most esteemed and versatile "men of letters." Whereas in 1983 he had published only a single dramatic work, a dramatization of one of his novels, Price now has six plays to his name, which are being produced in cities across the country, including San Francisco, New York, Cleveland, and Durham. In addition, the Price of 1983 was seemingly finished with the short story, not having written or published a single one since 1970, yet since the late 1980s he has added more than five hundred pages of short fiction to his oeuvre. The same is true in other genres, such as nonfiction prose, poetry, and translation; since 1983 Price has become a much more significant and imposing figure in each of these fields. Through this recent prolific burst, in which he has demonstrated extraordinary versatility and received lavish praise, Price has added bulk to his literary presence. For those who admire and value his work, he has indeed become a major American literary figure.

One could argue, however, that this new work, for all its immensity and variety, is not dramatically different from Price's earlier work. For instance, Price continues to explore and pursue many of the same themes; he persists in writing in a traditional, realistic mode which shares little with the experimentation of modernism and postmodernism; and he continues to set his work in the central North Carolina locale in which he has spent nearly all of his life. In addition, he even resurrects characters from works written before 1983—Rosacoke Mustian, Wesley Beavers, Grainger Walters, Hutch Mayfield. If Price's work has not changed in any sizable way since the 1960s and 1970s, why is it receiving so much more attention now than it did then?

Though his work has not changed in any *dramatic* fashion since 1983, there are differences which, along with changes in literary fashion, account for the increased attention. Most notably, Price has become less demanding of his readers, and more accessible. The Price of recent years would not begin a novel with a 192-word, serpentine sentence as he did in *A Long and Happy Life,* nor is it even likely he would impose upon his readers an epigraph in Italian or German as he did in his first three novels. Furthermore, it is not likely that Price would now generate a novel as literarily self-conscious as, say, *Love and Work.* The Price of recent years is less astringent and more inviting. Consider, for instance, the opening to *Love and Work,* which appeared in 1968:

> The phone's first ring pierced his study door, a klaxon vs. cheap birch veneer. . . . He stood between desk and door, hands clenched, jaws grating, while each ring screwed deeper into his absurd command, absurd resolve—general, tycoon, migrained duchess.

Now compare the opening sentences of a more recent novel, *Kate Vaiden:*

> The best thing about my life up to here is, nobody believes it. I stopped trying to make people hear it long ago, and I'm nothing but a real middle-sized white woman that has kept on going with strong eyes and teeth for fifty-seven years. You can touch me; I answer.

Whereas the former passage, with its poetic intensity, feels literary in nature, the latter sounds like an actual human voice. Since 1983, Price has written primarily in the first person, offering a variety of memorable and credible voices. The storytelling "I," the personal voice, has become dominant in Price's recent work: in his fiction (*Kate Vaiden, The Tongues of Angels, Blue Calhoun,* "The Enormous Door," "An Early Christmas"); in his nonfiction prose (*Clear Pictures, A Whole New Life, A Common Room*); and in his poetry (*The Laws of Ice, The Use of Fire*). In all his recent writings Price demonstrates his ability to generate and gracefully work a range of human voices; and particularly when he is composing in the voice of a late-middle-aged southern man or woman, his prose soars and becomes almost musical.

In addition to the change in Price's voice, his work has deepened and intensified because he has plunged more openly and personally into a cauldron of crucial matters regarding race, sexuality, religion, and gender. Though Price's work has long explored alternatives to heterosexual love and demonstrated that human sexuality is complex and resistant to social categorization, homo- and bisexuality were kept largely in the shadows of his work until the early 1980s. With novels like *The Source of Light, Good Hearts,* and *The Tongues of Angels,* though, Price brings homoeroticism to the forefront, and with *The Promise of Rest* in 1995, he goes further, offering his fullest and most candid exploration of homosexual desire. With *Promise,* Price provides a cast of characters who are predominantly homo- or bisexual and who speak quite candidly about their sexual lives—something not always possible in a southern genteel environment.

Price has also explored race in a slightly different manner in recent years, directly confronting such high-pitched emotional issues as racial hostility, interracial love, and the moral failure of white southerners to fight racial inequality. In *Clear Pictures,* Price discusses at length how both he and his family failed to actively resist and battle racial inequality, and of the burden of guilt they share because of that failure. And in such works as "The

MAN OF LETTERS

Fare to the Moon," *Full Moon,* and *The Promise of Rest,* Price closely examines interracial relationships and love. Though black-white relations play a significant role in such earlier works as *A Long and Happy Life* and *The Surface of Earth,* those novels do not actively explore and question the politics of racial division in the United States. *The Promise of Rest,* though, does, and it again expands Price's gallery of characters by offering Wyatt Bondurant, a northern-urban-black-militant-queer who speaks of racial revolution. Whereas Price's characters often sound like one another—with similarities in tone, dialect, diction, syntax, colloquialisms, and conversational interests—Wyatt is something new for Price: a voice from the outside, hostile to almost everything and everybody that one typically finds within Price's fictional world. Because of the contrast he provides, one wishes an even larger role for the Wyatt Bondurants in Price's future writings.

Another new direction in Price's recent work is the increased attention to disease and dying. Consider how many of his recent characters have been afflicted with life-threatening illness: Kate Vaiden has cervical cancer; Bridge Boatner is in a wheelchair (in "An Early Christmas"); Wade Mayfield and Wyatt Bondurant die of AIDS; Reynolds Price nearly dies of spinal cancer; Bob Barefoot dies of leukemia. Though it is natural to see the increased presence of disease, illness, and death in a writer's later work, Price's case is extreme due to his own illness. In his more recent work, beginning with *Blue Calhoun* and extending through *A Whole New Life* and *The Promise of Rest,* illness, death, deathbed scenes, and healing play an increasingly dominant role. One does not yet have a clear sense of where Price's experience with devastating illness will take his work, but it appears to be moving in this direction, and the results so far are nothing short of fascinating.

Where then does one place Reynolds Price in relation to other twentieth-century writers? Stephen Spender ranks him with Faulkner and Welty, and one would likely need to include, in regard to southerners, O'Connor, Porter, and Percy. While Price has not received the degree of critical attention that has been devoted to such contemporaries as Updike, Morrison, DeLillo, or Pynchon, that situation is changing. As his oeuvre expands and as his work deepens and intensifies, Price is becoming an increasingly significant presence in contemporary American literature.

In addition, as Rooke pointed out in 1983, one must continue to be vigilant concerning the "new directions his work may take." Another book of biblical translations and essays, *Three Gospels,* is to be published in 1996. And, says Price, "I do hope to turn soon to the completion of a new volume of poems . . . a new play . . . and a new novel. Beyond that more essays and perhaps another volume of memoir."[14] Should the prolific burst continue, in twelve more years one may again be looking at a rather different Reynolds Price. Though cultural circumstances and fashion have worked against his career, Price has endured—his first novel, written thirty-three years ago, has never been out of print—and with his recent extraordinary burst of creativity, his work is gaining a more widespread appreciation. It is, of course, impossible to determine which writers and works future generations will value; however, it would not at all be surprising to see Reynolds Price—given his immense and diverse body of work, and his bold and mysterious vision—emerge as one of the dominant literary figures of our time.

Chapter 1: Understanding Reynolds Price

1. Reynolds Price, *Clear Pictures* (New York: Atheneum, 1989) 29.

2. *Clear Pictures* 29.

3. *Clear Pictures* 30.

4. Cited in Frederick Busch, "The Art of Fiction CXXVII," *Paris Review* 33.121 (Winter 1991): 157.

5. Anne Tyler, "Reynolds Price: Duke of Writers," *Vanity Fair* 49.7 (July 1986): 82.

6. William S. Price, Jr., "Growing Up with Genius," *Reynolds Price: From "A Long and Happy Life" to "Good Hearts,"* ed. Sue Laslie Kimball and Lynn Veach Sadler (Fayetteville, NC: Methodist College P, 1989) 2.

7. Price, *Clear Pictures* 171.

8. *Clear Pictures* 171

9. Daniel Voll, "The Spy That Stayed: A Conversation with Reynolds Price," *Conversations with Reynolds Price,* ed. Jefferson Humphries (Jackson: UP of Mississippi, 1991) 166.

10. Josephine Humphreys, "Reynolds Price's Words Ring Sure and True," rev. of *A Common Room* and *A Long and Happy Life,* by Reynolds Price, *Atlanta Journal-Constitution* 7 Feb. 1988: J8.

11. Cited in Michael Ruhlman, "A Writer at His Best," *New York Times Magazine* 20 Sept. 1987: 133.

12. Michael Kreyling, "Reynolds Price," *The History of Southern Literature,* ed. Louis D. Rubin, Jr., et al. (Baton Rouge: Louisiana State UP, 1985) 521.

13. Humphries, introduction, *Conversations with Reynolds Price* viii.

14. Reynolds Price, *A Whole New Life* (New York: Atheneum, 1994) 28.

15. *A Whole New Life* 183.

16. *A Whole New Life* 189.

17. The collaboration between Price and Taylor goes back to 1982, when Taylor wrote the score for a PBS television production of Price's play *Private Contentment* (Taylor's wife, the actress Kathryn Walker, starred in the play). The first song which Price and Taylor wrote together was "Hymn" in 1988. Taylor had wanted to write a song for the retirement of an old friend, Bishop Paul Moore, and Price suggested they write a hymn. He then wrote the lyrics to "Hymn," which can be found in *The Use of Fire* (1990), and Taylor added the music (it was recorded several years later under the name "New Hymn" on Taylor's *Live* CD). The other song, "Copperline," which they cowrote in 1991 while Price was staying with Taylor at his Connecticut home, can be found on Taylor's *New Moon Shine* CD (Reynolds Price, personal interview, 26–28 August 1994).

18. Stephen Spender, critical blurb, dust jacket to first hardcover edition of *A Long and Happy Life* (New York: Atheneum, 1962), cited in Ruhlman 134; Jefferson Humphries, "'A Vast Common Room': Twenty-five Years of Essays and Fiction by Reynolds Price," *Southern Review* 24.3 (Summer 1988): 695; Lloyd Shaw, "'Blue' Raises Southern Life, Dialogue and People above Worn Cliches," review of *Blue Calhoun,* by Reynolds Price, *Washington Times* 7 June 1992: B8.

19. Kreyling, "Reynolds Price" 519.

20. John Wain, "Mantle of Faulkner?" rev. of *A Generous Man,* by Reynolds Price, *New Republic* 14 May 1966: 33

21. Benjamin DeMott, "A Minor Faulkner," rev. of *The Source of Light,* by Reynolds Price, *Saturday Review* 8.4 (Apr. 1981): 72.

22. For instance, one does not often speak of Roth or Updike as northeastern novelists, nor does one belittle their work for being derivative and second rate in comparison to, say, Melville, an imposing northeastern writer whose influence, at least upon Roth and Updike, is relatively insignificant. Because of the presence of Faulkner, mid- to

late-twentieth-century southern writers, unlike the writers of other U.S. regions, have been treated in a distinct and often disparaging manner by critics.

23. Reynolds Price, "Dodo, Phoenix, or Tough Old Cock," *A Common Room: Essays 1954–1987* (New York: Atheneum, 1987) 168–69.

24. Constance Rooke, *Reynolds Price* (Boston: Twayne, 1983) 12. Rooke has provided the most valuable commentary to date on Price's style; see 12–14.

25. Louis W. Chicatelli, "Family as Fate in Reynolds Price's *The Surface of Earth* and *The Source of Light,*" *Mid-Hudson Language Studies* 5 (1982): 130–31.

26. Humphries, "'A Vast Common Room'" 692; see also Rooke, *Reynolds Price* 10–12.

27. Fred Chappell, "Welcome to High Culture," *An Apple for My Teacher,* ed. Louis D. Rubin, Jr. (Chapel Hill: Algonquin, 1987) 14–28.

28. Price, "Dodo, Phoenix, or Tough Old Cock" 168.

29. Reynolds Price, preface to *Early Dark,* in *Full Moon and Other Plays* (New York: Theatre Communications Group, 1993) 4.

30. Clayton L. Eichelberger, "Reynolds Price: 'A Banner in Defeat,'" *Journal of Popular Culture* 1.2 (1967): 410–11.

31. William E. Ray, "Conversations: Reynolds Price and William Ray," *Conversations with Reynolds Price,* ed. Jefferson Humphries (Jackson: UP of Mississippi, 1991) 89.

32. Jefferson Humphries, "Feast Thy Heart: An Interview," *Conversations with Reynolds Price,* ed. Jefferson Humphries (Jackson: UP of Mississippi, 1991) 211.

33. Reynolds Price, "A Vast Common Room," *A Common Room: Essays 1954–1987* (New York: Atheneum, 1987) 374–75.

34. Wallace Kaufman, "Panel Discussion on *Private Contentment,*" *Reynolds Price: From "A Long and Happy Life" to "Good Hearts,"* ed. Sue Laslie Kimball and Lynn Veach Sadler (Fayetteville, NC: Methodist College P, 1989) 106.

35. Cited in "Reynolds Price," *World Authors 1950–1970,* ed. John Wakeman (New York: H. W. Wilson, 1975) 1166.

36. Wallace Kaufman, "Notice I'm Still Smiling: Reynolds Price," *Conversations with Reynolds Price,* ed. Jefferson Humphries (Jackson: UP of Mississippi, 1991) 17; Ray 96–97.

37. Ray 94.

38. Susan Ketchin, "Reynolds Price: Interview," *The Christ-Haunted Landscape* (Jackson: UP of Mississippi, 1994) 70.

39. Ketchin 70.

40. Price, *Clear Pictures* 234–35.

41. Reynolds Price, *The Tongues of Angels* (New York: Atheneum, 1990) 40.

42. Ketchin 82.

43. Reynolds Price, "At the Heart," *A Common Room: Essays 1954–1987* (New York: Atheneum, 1987) 405.

44. Reynolds Price, *A Palpable God* (New York: Atheneum, 1978) 13–14.

45. Ketchin 80.

46. Ketchin 79.

Chapter 2: The Mustian Novels

1. As Constance Rooke writes, "*Early Dark* serves to reveal the author's growing support of Wesley and his belief that Rosacoke is a flawed heroine." See Rooke, *Reynolds Price* (Boston: Twayne, 1983) 38.

2. Reynolds Price, *Clear Pictures* (New York: Atheneum, 1989) 172.

3. *Clear Pictures* 171.

4. Rooke, *Reynolds Price* 139.

5. Hiram Haydn, Price's editor then at Atheneum, explained in his memoir how he was unable at a sales conference "to convey this sense of [*A Long and Happy Life*'s] rareness." "Since no one believes me about

it," he continued, "I'm going to get endorsements from people whose names they will believe." See Haydn, *Words and Faces* (New York: Harcourt, 1974) 276.

6. Whitney Balliett, "Substance and Shadow," rev. of *A Long and Happy Life,* by Reynolds Price, *New Yorker* 38 (7 Apr. 1962): 180.

7. Balliett 178; rev. of *A Long and Happy Life,* by Reynolds Price, *Time* 23 Mar. 1962: 88.

8. Jay Tolson, "The Price of Grace," rev. of *A Common Room* and *Good Hearts,* by Reynolds Price, *New Republic* 4 July 1988: 34.

9. Michael Kreyling, "Fee, Fie, Faux Faulkner: Parody and Postmodernism in Southern Literature," *Southern Review* 29.1 (Winter 1993): 8.

10. Reynolds Price, personal interview, 26–28 August 1994.

11. Rooke, *Reynolds Price* 38.

12. Reynolds Price, "*A Long and Happy Life:* Fragments of Groundwork," *Virginia Quarterly Review* 41.2 (Spring 1965): 238.

13. "*A Long and Happy Life:* Fragments of Groundwork" 239.

14. Reynolds Price, *A Long and Happy Life* (New York: Atheneum, 1962) 175. Subsequent references are to this edition and are noted parenthetically.

15. Rooke, *Reynolds Price* 25.

16. Price, "*A Long and Happy Life:* Fragments of Groundwork" 240.

17. Dante, *Paradiso* 13.133–35, trans. Allen Mandelbaum (Berkeley: U of California P, 1984).

18. Allen Shepherd, "Love (and Marriage) in *A Long and Happy Life,*" *Twentieth Century Literature* 17 (January 1971): 29.

19. Reynolds Price, "To the Reader," *Things Themselves: Essays and Scenes* (New York: Atheneum, 1972) xiv. The essay "News for the Mineshaft: An Afterword to *A Generous Man*" appears in both *Things Themselves* and *A Common Room: Essays 1954–1987* (New York: Atheneum, 1987). All quoted passages from this essay are taken from the latter collection.

20. Price, "News for the Mineshaft" 49; Wallace Kaufman, "Notice, I'm Still Smiling: Reynolds Price," *Conversations with Reynolds Price,* ed. Jefferson Humphries (Jackson: UP of Mississippi, 1991) 13.

21. Price, "News for the Mineshaft" 47.

22. Daniel Frederick Daniel, "Within and Without a Region," diss., U of Wisconsin, 1977, 90.

23. Though it is suggested in *A Generous Man* that Milo achieves sexual consummation with Lois and Kate, *Good Hearts* provides what Price calls "an alternate version of the truth." In *Good Hearts* the middle-aged Milo admits to Wesley, "In my whole life . . . I touched one woman [Sissie]" (251). Is Milo then falsely boasting in *A Generous Man*? Or is he lying in *Good Hearts*? Price, who regards this as a form of narrative playfulness, prefers to let the reader deal with it. Another example of an alternate version of the truth concerns Wesley's military travels. In *A Long and Happy Life* it appears that Wesley has never been out of the country; however, in *Good Hearts* one is told that while in the military "he'd been to Gibraltar, Naples, Rome" (Price, personal interview, 26–28 August 1994).

24. In *Clear Pictures* Price writes of how the beginning of sexual maturity "led to my first extended and steady writing": "Blissfully astounded by these new carnal gifts, . . . I confessed them to one of those leather-bound five-year diaries. . . . I kept . . . a minutely attentive chart of my maturation, with drawings that were Germanic in the rapt care expended on every follicle, curl and vein, plus measurements (all of which I burned in 1958 on learning that I'd got my first full job, teaching the young)" (170).

25. Reynolds Price, *A Generous Man* (New York: Atheneum, 1966) 48. Subsequent references are to this edition and are noted parenthetically.

26. Price, "News for the Mineshaft" 42–47.

27. See Daniel 80–87; and Rooke, *Reynolds Price* 61.

28. Clayton L. Eichelberger, "Reynolds Price: 'A Banner in Defeat,'" *Journal of Popular Culture* 1.2 (1967): 411.

29. Price, "News for the Mineshaft" 49.

30. William E. Ray, "Conversations: Reynolds Price and William Ray," *Conversations with Reynolds Price,* ed. Jefferson Humphries (Jackson: UP of Mississippi, 1991) 98.

31. Price, "News for the Mineshaft" 52.

32. Terry Roberts, "Love and Work: The Art of Reynolds Price," *Conversations with Reynolds Price,* ed. Jefferson Humphries (Jackson: UP of Mississippi, 1991) 180.

33. Ray 98.

34. Price, "News for the Mineshaft" 46.

35. Ray 98.

36. Price, "News for the Mineshaft" 42.

37. Kaufman, "Notice, I'm Still Smiling" 16–17.

38. Reynolds Price, *A Whole New Life* (New York: Atheneum, 1994) 141.

39. *A Whole New Life* 141.

40. Jefferson Humphries, "Feast Thy Heart: An Interview," *Conversations with Reynolds Price,* ed. Jefferson Humphries (Jackson: UP of Mississippi, 1991) 214.

41. Reynolds Price, *Good Hearts* (New York: Atheneum, 1988) 109. Subsequent references are to this edition and are noted parenthetically.

42. Jefferson Humphries, "'A Vast Common Room': Twenty- five Years of Essays and Fiction by Reynolds Price," *Southern Review* 24.3 (Summer 1988): 689.

43. Monroe K. Spears, "Scenes from a Marriage," rev. of *Good Hearts,* by Reynolds Price, *Washington Post Book World* 10 Apr. 1988: 5.

44. Tolson 38.

45. Price, personal interview, 26–28 August 1994.

46. Vince Aletti, "A Song of Old Lovers: The Once and Future Reynolds Price," rev. of *Good Hearts,* by Reynolds Price, *Village Voice Literary Supplement* June 1988: 13.

47. Gail Caldwell, "Rosa and Wesley Halfway Home," rev. of

Good Hearts, by Reynolds Price, *Boston Globe* 10 Apr. 1988: A17.

48. Sven Birkerts, "Rape and Transfiguration," rev. of *Good Hearts* and *A Long and Happy Life,* by Reynolds Price, *Los Angeles Times Book Review* 22 May 1988: 3; Lee Lescaze, "The Seductions of Routine," rev. of *Good Hearts,* by Reynolds Price, *Wall Street Journal* 14 June 1988: 32.

Chapter 3: A Great Circle

1. Bryan Woolley, "Reynolds Price No Twig Cut from Faulkner's Tree," *Dallas Times Herald* 17 May 1981: P4.

2. From Reynolds Price, letter to James Schiff, 16 Sept. 1994.

3. Price discusses race in the chapter "Black Help" in his memoir *Clear Pictures* (New York: Atheneum, 1989) 83–119.

4. Reynolds Price, *The Promise of Rest* (New York: Scribner, 1995) 33.

5. Michael Brondoli, "Landscape of Exiles; Two Families in the South," rev. of *The Surface of Earth,* by Reynolds Price, *Providence Sunday Journal* 3 August 1975: H34; Michael Kreyling, "Reynolds Price," *The History of Southern Literature,* ed. Louis D. Rubin, Jr., et al. (Baton Rouge: Louisiana State UP, 1985) 521.

6. In 1973 Barth's *Chimera* actually tied for the award with John Williams's *Augustus,* and in 1974 Pynchon's *Gravity's Rainbow* tied with Isaac Bashevis Singer's *A Crown of Feathers and Other Stories.*

7. Richard Gilman, "A Mastodon of a Novel, by Reynolds Price," rev. of *The Surface of Earth,* by Reynolds Price, *New York Times Book Review* 29 June 1975: 1–2.

8. Eudora Welty, letter, *New York Times Book Review* 20 July 1975: 24–25; Richard Gilman, letter, *New York Times Book Review* 20 July 1975, 25; Shaun O'Connell, "American Fiction, 1975: Celebration in Wonderland," *Massachusetts Review* 17.1 (Spring 1976): 177–78.

9. Fred Chappell, "*The Surface of Earth,*" rev. of *The Surface of Earth,* by Reynolds Price, *Duke Alumni Register* 62.1 (Oct. 1975): 6.

10. Reynolds Price, *The Surface of Earth* (New York: Atheneum, 1975) 394–95; subsequent references are to this edition and are noted parenthetically.

11. Fred Chappell, "*The Surface of Earth:* A Pavement of Good Intentions," rev. of *The Surface of Earth,* by Reynolds Price, *Archive* 88.1 (Fall 1975): 77.

12. Constance Rooke, "On Women and His Own Work: An Interview with Reynolds Price," *Southern Review* 14 (October 1978): 706–25. Reprinted in *Conversations with Reynolds Price,* ed. Jefferson Humphries (Jackson: UP of Mississippi, 1991) 154.

13. Constance Rooke, *Reynolds Price* (Boston: Twayne, 1983) 12–13.

14. Christopher Lehmann-Haupt, "A History of the South," rev. of *The Surface of Earth,* by Reynolds Price, *New York Times* 18 July 1975: 29.

15. Cited in Harriet Doar, "Price's Novel Embraces Armful of Years," *Charlotte Observer* 20 July 1975: 4B.

16. Reynolds Price, "Given Time: Beginning *The Surface of Earth,*" *Antaeus* 21–22 (Spring–Summer 1976): 58.

17. Rooke, "On Women and His Own Work: An Interview with Reynolds Price" 158.

18. For commentary on Price's use of dreams in *The Surface of Earth* see Rooke, *Reynolds Price* 129–30; William Merritt Singer, "Revelation as Grace: A Study of the Twenty-two Dreams in Reynolds Price's *The Surface of Earth,*" master's thesis, U of North Carolina at Chapel Hill, 1977; and Roy Calhoun Fuller III, "The Sleeping Giant: Dreams and Artistry in the Fictions of Reynolds Price," diss., Northwestern U, 1990. Also see Reynolds Price, *Writers Dreaming,* ed. Naomi Epel (New York: Carol Southern, 1973) 200–08.

19. Ernest Jones, *On the Nightmare* (London: Hogarth, 1931) 44. Though other psychologists since Jones—for instance, J. A. Hadfield, Roger Broughton, Henri Gastaut, and John Mack—have expanded upon and pushed the study of the incubus/nightmare further, Jones's work, as

David Hufford points out, "has had a great and lasting influence" and is still significant. See Hufford, *The Terror That Comes in the Night* (Philadelphia: U of Pennsylvania P, 1982) 135.

20. Jones 75–76; Reynolds Price, "A Vast Common Room," *A Common Room: Essays 1954–1987* (New York: Atheneum, 1987) 374.

21. Lee Yopp, "Panel Discussion," *Reynolds Price: From "A Long and Happy Life" to "Good Hearts,"* ed. Sue Laslie Kimball and Lynn Veach Sadler (Fayetteville, NC: Methodist College P, 1989) 105.

22. Reynolds Price, *The Source of Light* (New York: Atheneum, 1981) 6.

23. Reynolds Price, *The Source of Light* (New York: Atheneum, 1981) 184. Subsequent references are to this edition and are noted parenthetically.

24. *Love and Work* is set in an *unspecified* locale, which may or may not be the South.

25. John Updike, *Picked-Up Pieces* (New York: Knopf, 1975) 504.

26. Though Price states that nine months pass, I count only eight.

27. Later in Rome, Hutch will visit Michelangelo's statue of the risen Christ.

28. Price, *Clear Pictures* 298–99.

29. Joyce Carol Oates, "Portrait of the Artist as Son, Lover, Elegist," rev. of *The Source of Light,* by Reynolds Price, *New York Times Book Review* 26 Apr. 1981: 30.

30. Reynolds Price, personal interview, 26–28 August 1994.

31. Price, personal interview, 26–28 August 1994.

32. Louis W. Chicatelli, "Family as Fate in Reynolds Price's *The Surface of Earth* and *The Source of Light,*" *Mid-Hudson Language Studies* 5 (1982): 133.

33. Reynolds Price, *The Promise of Rest* (New York: Scribner, 1995) 13. Subsequent references are to this edition and are noted parenthetically. My commentary on *Promise,* written prior to the pub-

lication of the novel, was dependent upon a typed manuscript and a later "advance reading copy" of the work.

Chapter 4: Artists and Outlaws

1. Susan Ketchin, "Reynolds Price: Interview," *The Christ-Haunted Landscape: Faith and Doubt in Southern Fiction* (Jackson: UP of Mississippi, 1994) 97.

2. Ketchin 99.

3. Rosellen Brown, "Travels with a Dangerous Woman," rev. of *Kate Vaiden,* by Reynolds Price, *New York Times Book Review* 29 June 1986: 1.

4. Jefferson Humphries notes, though, that the heroines of these two novels, Kate Vaiden and Rosacoke Mustian, are "polar opposite[s]." Whereas Rosacoke possesses a "fierce loyalty" and an "unswerving commitment," Kate betrays and abandons those whom she loves. See Humphries, "'A Vast Common Room': Twenty-five Years of Essays and Fiction by Reynolds Price," *Southern Review* 24.3 (Summer 1988): 691–92.

5. Reynolds Price, *Kate Vaiden* (New York: Atheneum, 1986) 216. Subsequent references are to this edition and are noted parenthetically.

6. Jefferson Humphries, "Feast Thy Heart: An Interview," *Conversations with Reynolds Price,* ed. Jefferson Humphries (Jackson: UP of Mississippi, 1991) 211.

7. Joseph Dewey, "A Time to Bolt: Suicide, Androgyny, and the Dislocation of the Self in Reynolds Price's *Kate Vaiden,*" *Mississippi Quarterly* 45.1 (Winter 1991–1992): 17.

8. The version of the essay that appeared in the *New York Times* was called "Men Creating Women," a title which Price had not chosen and which he felt was a "combative flag to fly over an essay whose main intention is to tend the deeper wounds of gender warfare" (Preface, *A Common Room,* xii). A revised version of the essay, from which I have

quoted, is titled "A Vast Common Room"; it appears in Price's collection of essays, *A Common Room: Essays 1954–1987* (New York: Atheneum, 1987), 371–77.

9. Brown 41.

10. Edith T. Hartin, "Reading as a Woman: Reynolds Price and Creative Androgyny in *Kate Vaiden*," *Southern Quarterly* 29.3 (Spring 1991): 48, 51.

11. Dewey 24.

12. Price, "A Vast Common Room" 377.

13. Humphries, "Feast Thy Heart" 214.

14. "Feast Thy Heart" 213.

15. Another companion piece to *Blue Calhoun* is Price's short story "Serious Need" (from his *Collected Stories*), which was written as a practice sketch for the novel Price knew he was going to write.

16. Steve Brzezinski, rev. of *Blue Calhoun,* by Reynolds Price, *Antioch Review* 50 (Fall 1992): 771; Melinda Ruley, "Amazing Grace," rev. of *Blue Calhoun,* by Reynolds Price, *Independent Weekly* [Durham, NC] 20 May 1992: 24; Janet Byrne, "An Old- School Rake and His Teen Muse," rev. of *Blue Calhoun,* by Reynolds Price, *Wall Street Journal* 26 June 1992: A9; Dannye Romine, "The Colors of Blue Calhoun," rev. of *Blue Calhoun,* by Reynolds Price, *Charlotte Observer* 3 May 1992: 5C.

17. See Michiko Kakutani, "Shocking Confessions to Send a Grandchild," rev. of *Blue Calhoun,* by Reynolds Price, *New York Times* 8 May 1992: C28; Robert Towers, "June and January in Raleigh, N.C.," rev. of *Blue Calhoun,* by Reynolds Price, *New York Times Book Review* 24 May 1992: 10; Susan Wood, "Blue Moon of Carolina," rev. of *Blue Calhoun,* by Reynolds Price, *Washington Post* 10 May 1992: 5; Michael Coffey, "Southern Discomfort," rev. of *Blue Calhoun,* by Reynolds Price, *Los Angeles Times* 21 June 1992: 12.

18. Kakutani C28.

19. Reynolds Price, *Blue Calhoun* (New York: Atheneum, 1992) 110. Subsequent references are to this edition and are noted parenthetically.

20. One could read Dane as Blue's doppelgänger—a darker, more silent, and more tragic twin to Blue.

21. Towers 10, Wood 5.

22. Irving Malin, rev. of *Blue Calhoun,* by Reynolds Price, *Southern Quarterly* 31.3 (Spring 1993): 123; Dale Neal, "Reynolds Price Returns with Tale of Passion," rev. of *Blue Calhoun,* by Reynolds Price, *Asheville Citizen-Times* 31 May 1992: 6L; Charles Sermon, "A Powerful Tug," rev. of *Blue Calhoun,* by Reynolds Price, *State* [Columbia, SC] 10 May 1992: 4F.

23. Cited in Don O'Briant, "Prolific Price Ignores Critics, Does It His Way," *Atlanta Journal and Constitution* 14 June 1992: N10.

24. Though much of *The Source of Light* takes place in Europe, approximately half of the novel is set in a very specific southern locale.

25. William E. Ray, "Conversations: Reynolds Price and William Ray," *Conversations with Reynolds Price,* ed. Jefferson Humphries (Jackson: UP of Mississippi, 1991) 92–93.

26. Ray 91.

27. Ray 92.

28. Granville Hicks, "To Whom Does a Man Belong?" rev. of *Love and Work,* by Reynolds Price, *Saturday Review* 25 May 1968: 18.

29. "Question Marks," rev. of *Love and Work,* by Reynolds Price, *Times Literary Supplement* 5 December 1968: 1357.

30. "Finding Work" first appeared in Duke University's *Chanticleer* and later in Price's collected essays *A Common Room: Essays 1954–1987* (New York: Atheneum, 1987) 15–19.

31. Humphries, "Feast Thy Heart" 201; William S. Price, Jr., "Growing Up with Genius," *Reynolds Price: From "A Long and Happy Life" to "Good Hearts,"* ed. Sue Laslie Kimball and Lynn Veach Sadler (Fayetteville, NC: Methodist College P, 1989) 3.

32. Humphries, "Feast Thy Heart" 202.

33. Reynolds Price, *Love and Work* (New York: Atheneum, 1968) 3. Subsequent references are to this edition and are noted parenthetically.

34. Humphries, "Feast Thy Heart" 251.

35. Reynolds Price, *Clear Pictures* (New York: Atheneum, 1989) 301.

36. G. M. Holland, trans., *Die Frau ohne Schatten* (London: Decca Record Co., 1992), act 1.

37. Reynolds Price, *A Whole New Life* (New York: Atheneum, 1994) 160. Price writes that his memoir *Clear Pictures* was also "pried" from him by hypnosis.

38. *A Whole New Life* 161.

39. *A Whole New Life* 161–62; *Clear Pictures* 10.

40. One of Price's best and most visual short stories, "An Early Christmas" (from his *Collected Stories*), also utilizes Bridge Boatner as a narrator. The story revolves around Bridge's visit to Jerusalem.

41. Reynolds Price, personal interview, 26–28 August 1994.

42. Price, *Clear Pictures* 10.

43. Ketchin 70.

44. Reynolds Price, *The Tongues of Angels* (New York: Atheneum, 1990) 29–30. Subsequent references are to this edition and are noted parenthetically.

Chapter 5: Man of Letters

1. Guy Davenport, "Doomed, Damned—and Unaware," rev. of *Permanent Errors,* by Reynolds Price, *New York Times Book Review* 11 Oct. 1970: 4; Ron Carlson, *"The Collected Stories of Reynolds Price,"* rev. of *The Collected Stories,* by Reynolds Price, *Southern Review* 30.2 (Apr. 1994): 371.

2. Stephen Spender, critical blurb, *Clear Pictures* (New York: Ballantine, 1990) ii.

3. Anthony Burgess, "Good Books," rev. of *A Palpable God,* by Reynolds Price, *New York Times Book Review* 12 Mar. 1978: 22; Frank Kermode, "Deciphering the Big Book," rev. of *A Palpable God,* by Reynolds Price, *New York Review of Books* 29 June 1978: 42.

4. David Patrick Stearns, "*New Music* Rings with Promise," *USA Today* 20 Oct. 1989: 5D.

5. Spender ii.

6. Robert Atwan, "The Territory Behind: Mark Twain and His Autobiographies," *Located Lives: Place and Idea in Southern Autobiography,* ed. J. Bill Berry (Athens: U of Georgia P, 1990) 45.

7. Reynolds Price, *Clear Pictures* (New York: Atheneum, 1989) 41. Subsequent references are to this edition and are noted parenthetically.

8. Reynolds Price, "The Thing Itself," *A Common Room* (New York: Atheneum, 1987) 13–14.

9. Reynolds Price, *A Whole New Life* (New York: Atheneum, 1994) 180. Subsequent references are to this edition and are noted parenthetically.

10. William A. Henry III, "The Mind Roams Free," *Time* 23 May 1994: 66.

11. In his review of *A Whole New Life,* Arthur W. Frank questions Price's failure to find useful books on illness. Frank writes, "Either [Price] missed the pertinent books or he disqualified those he found. By 1984 those who had written about their illnesses included Stewart Alsop, Cornelius Ryan, Audre Lorde, May Sarton and Fitzhugh Mullan. . . ." Frank then goes on to suggest that "Price's disregard of other books might be what he needs to keep his experience radically personal." See Frank, "*A Whole New Life: An Illness and a Healing,*" rev. of *A Whole New Life,* by Reynolds Price, *Christian Century* 23 Nov. 1994: 1108.

12. Richard Selzer, "Surviving," rev. of *A Whole New Life,* by Reynolds Price, *Los Angeles Times Book Review* 22 May 1994: 1.

13. Constance Rooke, *Reynolds Price* (Boston: Twayne, 1983) 145.

14. From Reynolds Price to James Schiff, 4 May 1995.

BIBLIOGRAPHY

Works by Reynolds Price

Novels

A Long and Happy Life. New York: Atheneum, 1962. London: Chatto and Windus, 1962.

A Generous Man. New York: Atheneum, 1966. London: Chatto and Windus, 1967.

Love and Work. New York: Atheneum, 1968. London: Chatto and Windus, 1968.

The Surface of Earth. New York: Atheneum, 1975. London: Arlington, 1977.

The Source of Light. New York: Atheneum, 1981.

Mustian: Two Novels and a Story [*A Long and Happy Life, A Generous Man,* "A Chain of Love"]. New York: Atheneum, 1983.

Kate Vaiden. New York: Atheneum, 1986. London: Chatto and Windus, 1987.

Good Hearts. New York: Atheneum, 1988.

The Tongues of Angels. New York: Atheneum, 1990.

Blue Calhoun. New York: Atheneum, 1992.

The Promise of Rest. New York: Scribner, 1995.

Collections of Short Stories

The Names and Faces of Heroes. New York: Atheneum, 1963. London: Chatto and Windus, 1963.

Permanent Errors. New York: Atheneum, 1970. London: Chatto and Windus, 1971.

The Foreseeable Future. New York: Atheneum, 1991.

The Collected Stories. New York: Atheneum, 1993.

BIBLIOGRAPHY

Collections of Poetry

Vital Provisions. New York: Atheneum, 1982.
The Laws of Ice. New York: Atheneum, 1987.
The Use of Fire. New York: Atheneum, 1990.

Memoirs

Clear Pictures: First Loves, First Guides. New York: Atheneum, 1989.
A Whole New Life: An Illness and a Healing. New York: Atheneum, 1994.

Plays

Early Dark. New York: Atheneum, 1977. Three acts, adapted from *A Long and Happy Life* and first produced at the WPA Theater, April 1978.
Private Contentment. New York: Atheneum, 1984. Written for *American Playhouse,* PBS, April 1982.
New Music: A Trilogy. New York: Theatre Communications Group, 1990. Includes *August Snow, Night Dance,* and *Better Days. August Snow* was commissioned for Hendrix College (Arkansas) drama students and performed fall 1985; the entire trilogy first was produced at Cleveland Play House, fall 1989.
Full Moon and Other Plays. New York: Theatre Communications Group, 1993. Includes two previously published plays, *Early Dark* and *Private Contentment;* the play *Full Moon* was commissioned for Duke University drama students and performed November 1988.

Collections of Nonfiction

Things Themselves: Essays and Scenes. New York: Atheneum, 1972.
A Common Room: Essays 1954–1987. New York: Atheneum, 1987.

BIBLIOGRAPHY

Translation

A Palpable God: Thirty Stories Translated from the Bible with an Essay on the Origins and Life of Narrative. New York: Atheneum, 1978.

Interviews

Busch, Frederick. "Reynolds Price: The Art of Fiction CXXVII." *Paris Review* 33.121 (Winter 1991): 150–79.

Humphries, Jefferson, ed. *Conversations with Reynolds Price.* Jackson: UP of Mississippi, 1991. Important collection of interviews.

Ketchin, Susan. "Reynolds Price: Interview." *The Christ- Haunted Landscape: Faith and Doubt in Southern Fiction.* Jackson: UP of Mississippi, 1994. 69–99. Rpt. of "Narrative Hunger and Silent Witness: An Interview with Reynolds Price." *Georgia Review* 47 (Fall 1993): 522–42.

Ray, William E. "Conversations: Reynolds Price and William Ray." *Conversations with Reynolds Price.* Ed. Jefferson Humphries. Jackson: UP of Mississippi, 1991. 54–138. Rpt. of *Conversations: Reynolds Price and William Ray.* Mississippi Valley Collection 9. Memphis: Memphis State, 1976.

Selected Works about Price

Bibliography

Kimball, Sue Laslie, and Lynn Veach Sadler, eds., "Bibliography." *Reynolds Price: From "A Long and Happy Life" to "Good Hearts," with a Bibliography.* Fayetteville, NC: Methodist College P, 1989.

Wright, Stuart, and James L. W. West III. *Reynolds Price: A Bibliography 1949–1984.* Charlottesville: UP of Virginia, 1986. Detailed record of Price's primary works.

BIBLIOGRAPHY

Books

Kimball, Sue Laslie, and Lynn Veach Sadler, eds. *Reynolds Price: From "A Long and Happy Life" to "Good Hearts," with a Bibliography.* Fayetteville, NC: Methodist College P, 1989. From the proceedings of the Seventh Annual Southern Writers' Symposium held at Methodist College, April 15–16, 1988—a collection of critical and biographical essays, and a comprehensive list of primary and secondary works. Extremely useful.

Rooke, Constance. *Reynolds Price.* Twayne's United States Authors Series 450. Boston: Twayne, 1983. The most valuable work on Price to date. An intelligent and thorough overview of his work through 1981.

Schiff, James A., ed., *Critical Essays on Reynolds Price.* G. K. Hall Critical Essays on American Literature. Boston: G. K. Hall, forthcoming, 1998.

Essays and Selected Reviews

Athas, Daphne. "Stars in the Work of Reynolds Price." Kimball and Sadler 14–23. Biographical and critical overview of Price.

Barnes, Daniel. "The Names and Faces of Reynolds Price." *Kentucky Review* 2.2 (1968): 76–91. A study of how Price explores the concept of identity through his deep concern with "names" and "faces."

Binding, Paul. "Reynolds Price." *Separate Country: A Literary Journey through the American South.* 2d ed. Jackson: UP of Mississippi, 1988. 157–91. Combines appreciative critical reading of Price's novels with a visit to Price's home.

Burgess, Anthony. "Good Books." *New York Times Book Review* 12 Mar. 1978: 13–14+. Favorable review of *A Palpable God.*

Chappell, Fred. *"The Surface of Earth:* A Pavement of Good Intentions." *Archive* 88.1 (Fall 1975): 75–82. Appreciative review-essay which offers excellent treatment of Price's prose style and dialogue.

BIBLIOGRAPHY

————. "Welcome to High Culture." *An Apple for My Teacher.* Ed. Louis Rubin, Jr. Chapel Hill: Algonquin, 1987. 14–28. Personal recollection of Price as editor of college literary magazine.

Chicatelli, Louis W. "Family as Fate in Reynolds Price's *The Surface of Earth* and *The Source of Light.*" *Mid-Hudson Language Studies* 5 (1982): 129–36.

Ciuba, Gary M. "The Discords and Harmonies of Love: Reynolds Price's *New Music.*" *Southern Quarterly* 29.2 (Winter 1991): 115–30. Argues that Price's imagination gravitates toward the dramatic and views the trilogy as literal music, "a score for voices."

————. "Price's *Love and Work:* Discovering the 'Perfect Story.'" *Renascence* 44.1 (Fall 1991): 45–60. A close reading which considers Thomas Eborn as a storyteller not in touch with Price's sacred and crucial demands for narrative.

Claxon, William N., Jr. "With This Ring, I Thee Wed." Kimball and Sadler 31–45.

Daniel, Daniel Frederick. "Amazing Crossroads in *Love and Work.*" Kimball and Sadler 46–53. Draws connections between *Love and Work* and Price's earlier work; considers how Eborn wills himself into painful isolation, then attempts to escape.

Davenport, Guy. "Doomed, Damned—and Unaware: *Permanent Errors.*" *New York Times Book Review* 11 Oct. 1970: 4. Significant review.

Dewey, Joseph. "A Time to Bolt: Suicide, Androgyny, and the Dislocation of the Self in Reynolds Price's *Kate Vaiden.*" *Mississippi Quarterly* 45.1 (Winter 1991–1992): 9–28. Valuable essay arguing that Kate rebels against the prescribed female role and defines herself in masculine stereotypes.

Eichelberger, Clayton L. "Reynolds Price: 'A Banner in Defeat.'" *Journal of Popular Culture* 1.2 (1967): 410–17. Discusses how Price's characters are meant to frustrate reader expectation; finds Price's first three books more ironic and pessimistic than most early critics do.

BIBLIOGRAPHY

Fuller, R. C. "Lunging in the Dark: Blindness and Vision, Disappointment and Aspiration in Reynolds Price's Trilogy." *Southern Quarterly* 33.2–3 (Winter–Spring 1995): 45–56. Considers vital role of audience as witness in *New Music* and examines the process by which Neal Avery transforms himself and realizes a vision of hope.

Gilman, Richard. "A Mastodon of a Novel, by Reynolds Price." *New York Times Book Review* 29 June 1975: 1–2. Controversial review of *The Surface of Earth* which acknowledges Price's abilities yet finds the novel to be out of touch with contemporary literary fashion.

Gurganus, Allan. *"The Surface of Earth." Washington Post Book World* 13 July 1975: 1–2. Favorable review.

Hartin, Edith T. "Reading as a Woman: Reynolds Price and Creative Androgyny in *Kate Vaiden." Southern Quarterly* 29.3 (Spring 1991): 37–52. A feminist reading of *Kate Vaiden* contending that Kate's voice and characterization are actually the products of a masculine tradition.

Henry, William A., III. "The Mind Roams Free." *Time* 23 May 1994: 66–68. Both a biographical piece on Price's bout with cancer and a review of *A Whole New Life.*

Humphries, Jefferson. "'A Vast Common Room': Twenty-five Years of Essays and Fiction by Reynolds Price." *Southern Review* 24.3 (Summer 1988): 686–95. Valuable, appreciative review-essay of five books by Price.

———. "Taking Things Seriously: Reynolds Price as Teacher and Writer." *Southwest Review* 74.1 (Winter 1989): 10–24. An eloquent essay and personal recollection which draws a connection between Price's teaching and writing, revealing in both a generous but demanding seriousness.

Jones, Gloria G. "Reynolds Price's *A Long and Happy Life:* Style and the Dynamics of Power." *CEA Critic* 56.1 (Fall 1993): 77–85. Detailed exploration of the relationship between language, gender, and power in Price's first novel.

BIBLIOGRAPHY

Kaufman, Wallace. "Portrait of the Artist as a Young Voyeur." Kimball and Sadler 7–13. Biographical and critical piece from Price's friend.

Kimball, Sue Laslie. "Reynolds Price, Biblical Scholar: 'Validation in the Narrative Bones.'" Kimball and Sadler 61–68.

Kreyling, Michael. "Motion and Rest in the Novels of Reynolds Price." *Southern Review* 16 (1980): 853–68. Excellent discussion of how *The Surface of Earth* engages in debate with Augustine's *Confessions.* Also examines the tension between the impulses of motion and rest in Price's first four novels.

———. "Reynolds Price." *The History of Southern Literature.* Ed. Louis D. Rubin, Jr., et al. Baton Rouge: Louisiana State UP, 1985. 519–22. A brief but brilliant overview of Price and his critical reception. Reprinted in Kimball and Sadler.

Oates, Joyce Carol. "Portrait of the Artist as Son, Lover, Elegist." *New York Times Book Review* 26 Apr. 1981: 3+. Favorable review of *The Source of Light.*

Orr, Linda. "The Duplicity of the Southern Story: Reflections on Reynolds Price's *The Surface of Earth* and Eudora Welty's 'The Wide Net.'" *South Atlantic Quarterly* 91.1 (Winter 1992): 111–37. Concentrates on the opening front-porch scene in *Surface* to demonstrate the guile and duplicity inherent in the Southern storytelling tradition.

Price, Reynolds. "Given Time: Beginning *The Surface of Earth.*" *Antaeus* 21–22 (Spring–Summer 1976): 57–64. Excerpts from Price's notebook for *The Surface of Earth.*

———. "*A Long and Happy Life:* Fragments of Groundwork." *Virginia Quarterly Review* 41.2 (Spring 1965): 236–47. Excerpts from Price's notebook for *A Long and Happy Life.*

Price, William S., Jr. "Growing Up with Genius." Kimball and Sadler 1–6. Biographical piece from Price's brother.

Ruhlman, Michael. "A Writer at His Best." *New York Times Magazine* 20 Sept. 1987: 60–61+. Biographical essay and overview.

BIBLIOGRAPHY

Sadler, Lynn Veach. "The 'Mystical Grotesque' in the Life and Works of Reynolds Price." *Southern Literary Journal* 21.2 (Spring 1989): 27–40. Discusses presence of the Southern Gothic and the grotesque in *The Surface of Earth* and *The Source of Light.*

———. "Reynolds Price and Religion: The 'Almost Blindingly Lucid, Palpable World.'" *Southern Quarterly* 26.2 (1988): 1–11. Considers role of God, religion, biblical narrative, and the mystical in Price's work and life; demonstrates how Price "charges" the natural world with meaning.

———. "'Small Calm Pleasures': The Mustians Revisited in Reynolds Price's *Good Hearts.*" Kimball and Sadler 72–83. A close reading which pays particular attention to character and language.

Schiff, James A. "Fathers and Sons in the Fiction of Reynolds Price: A Sense of Crucial Ambiguity." *Southern Review* 29.1 (Winter 1993): 16–29. Discusses the mysterious, charged eroticism between fathers and sons in Price's work; argues that Price's vision is bold and deserving of greater attention.

Shelton, Frank K. "The Family in Reynolds Price's *Kate Vaiden.*" Kimball and Sadler 84–90.

Shepherd, Allen. "Love (and Marriage) in *A Long and Happy Life.*" *Twentieth Century Literature* 17 (January 1971): 29–35. A useful discussion of Price's first novel which directs attention to the epigraph, the gesture of gift-giving, sucking/pulling imagery, and references to the novel's title.

———. "*Love and Work* and the Unseen World." *Topic* 12.23 (1972): 52–57.

———. "Notes on Nature in the Fiction of Reynolds Price." *Critique: Studies in Modern Fiction* 15.2 (1970): 83–94. Discusses the relationship between nature and humans in Price's first five books.

Stevenson, John W. "The Faces of Reynolds Price's Short Fiction." *Studies in Short Fiction* 3 (1965–1966): 300–06. Considers the "obligations of love" in Price's first collection of stories.

BIBLIOGRAPHY

Tolson, Jay. "The Price of Grace." *New Republic* 4 July 1988: 34–39. Valuable, mostly appreciative review of *Good Hearts* and *A Common Room* which provides an overview of Price's work.

Tyler, Anne. "Reynolds Price: Duke of Writers." *Vanity Fair* 49.7 (July 1986): 82–85. Biographical essay from the novelist and former Price student.

Vauthier, Simone. "The 'Circle in the Forest': Fictional Space in Reynolds Price's *A Long and Happy Life*." *Mississippi Quarterly* 28 (Spring 1975): 123–46. Intelligent discussion of space, nature, place, stasis, and movement in Price's first novel.

Wain, John. "Mantle of Faulkner?" *New Republic* 14 May 1966: 31–33. Negative review of *A Generous Man* which casts Price as an imitator of Faulkner.

Welty, Eudora. Letter. *New York Times Book Review* 20 July 1975: 24–25. Response to Gilman's negative review of *The Surface of Earth*.

Films about Reynolds Price

Clear Pictures. Dir. Charles Guggenheim. Direct Cinema, 1994.

Reynolds Price: A Writer's Inheritance. Dir. Marcia Rock. New York U Journalism Dept., 1986.

The Roots of Solitude: The Life and Work of Reynolds Price. Carolina Video, 1992.

INDEX

Page numbers in bold type denote extended discussion.

INDEX

INDEX

INDEX

INDEX

INDEX

INDEX

INDEX

INDEX

INDEX

Library of Congress Cataloging-in-Publication Data

Schiff, James A., 1958–
    Understanding Reynolds Price / James A. Schiff.
        p.   cm.— (Understanding contemporary American literature)
    Includes bibliographical references and index.
    ISBN 1–57003–126–6
    1. Price, Reynolds, 1933–   —Criticism and interpretation.
I. Title. II. Series.
PS3566.R54Z9 1996
813'.54—dc20   96–9971